TAKING THE TIDE

My Family's Ebb and Flow in Rockport, Texas
as told to Sue Hastings

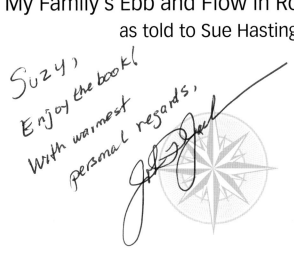

Suzy,
Enjoy the book!
With warmest
personal regards,

JOHN PORTER JACKSON

Front Cover:
Aerial view of Rockport Harbor

First printing 2011
Copyright © 2011 John Porter Jackson

ISBN 978-0-615-46771-9

Published by John Porter Jackson

Managing Editor: John Porter Jackson
Contributing Editor: Sue Hastings
Printing: Grunwald Printing Company, Corpus Christi, Texas, USA
Book design and production: Martell Speigner

There is a tide in the affairs of men,

Which, taken at the flood, leads on to fortune;

Omitted, all the voyage of their life

Is bound in shallows and in miseries.

On such a full sea are we now afloat;

And we must take the current when it serves,

Or lose our ventures.

William Shakespeare

Julius Caesar, Act IV, Sc. 3

TABLE OF CONTENTS

PREFACE

This slim volume chronicles hefty topics—feast and famine, hard work, core values, family heritage, determination, perseverance, focus, and striving to make a difference in one little corner of the world.

I'm the fifth generation of my family to live in Rockport, Texas, and I suppose I could have left this little town any time I wanted to. Certainly I had the education and the ambition to do so, but I've always felt, and often asked others: "Once you're here, why would you ever want to leave?"

Rockport and neighboring Fulton make up a modest resort-type community in tiny Aransas County. We have little industry but, as if to make up for that seeming lack, we have been blessed with unique charm and a rich history. I don't think there's a coastal town comparable to Rockport from Brownsville to Key West.

Because this town is small, many citizens have found, over the years, that they had to leave to make a decent living. I've been fortunate enough to stay because I grew up in a family business that started around the turn of the last century. My parents, grandparents, great-grandparents, and great-great-grandparents—model citizens of good stock—developed a rich family heritage and a commendable reputation. Much of this book is about our early years—family history, my growing up in the 1950s-60s, and then seventeen years of "taking the tide" while in the family business. That period included the good old days of the prosperous 1970s and then, when the tide went out, a plunge—literally to survival mode—through the 1980s.

Fortunately, I was able to move into a career that allowed me to stay in Rockport. I have prospered in this grand old place, enjoying a very successful profession in the financial services industry.

I did not focus on this field while I was in school; I never gave any thought to taking this fork in the road. Although I think I have above-average intelligence, many of my peers and colleagues are much smarter than I. But I suspect there are very few who work harder than I, and I doubt there is another individual in the entire financial services industry who transited from hard times in the shrimping business to success as an investment advisor.

People are willing to trust and do business with a advisor once they figure out who that person really is as an individual. That's a time-consuming process, but it results in strong and lasting relationships. I think my success derives largely from the story I have to tell. My clients take comfort from knowing that I arrived here through the school of hard knocks. They understand that the drive it took for me to get here is the drive I will employ in representing their financial interests. The character and integrity that have made me who I am are attributes that I will exercise in their advocacy.

Over the years, as I've told my story, I've heard again and again the same response: "You should write a book about all of that." So here it is. Perhaps this narrative will give you an idea of what makes me tick, an understanding of what is important to me, and a glimpse into a past that launched me down this unusual path.

The work ethic and drive and perseverance that my parents passed on to me have served me well in my successful second career. I am blessed, fortunate and thankful to have had a loving, supportive wife, great kids, and a wonderful extended family all along the journey. I look forward to continuing the adventure.

I believe that in the final analysis, it's not about how much wealth we can accumulate. Our most important asset is our name and the intrinsic value of what we can give back. I only hope and pray that my kids, grandkids and those who follow will continue to honor this heritage, maturing the assets molded and developed by preceding generations.

TAKING THE TIDE

PART I

OUR VENTURES

There is a tide . . .

I sit at my mahogany desk, in a comfortable chair, studying a computer screen that brings the world to me. Antique photographs, and current ones of my grandchildren, decorate the walls and a credenza. Awards hang on the wall too, but on sultry summer days in Rockport, my air conditioned office seems the ultimate prize for a job well done. I have not always enjoyed such comfort.

I contemplate a newspaper page, framed and hanging on my office wall. It's from our local paper, *The Rockport Pilot*, dated June 5, 1991, and the headline reads:

THE END OF AN ERA

A photograph fills a significant portion of the page, showing a shrimp boat, her stern toward the camera. She was one of my family's boats, and we had named her for my grandmother, Irene Norvell Jackson. On this day, the Jacksons were leaving the seafood business after three quarters of a century, and *Irene J* represents the last boat out of the harbor.

As I look at that picture, Shakespeare's words come to mind, and I nod in agreement. There is, indeed, a tide in the affairs of men.

 During most of my life, Texas had several big shrimp ports. There was a sizeable fleet at Brownsville/Port Isabel. Moving up the coast, the combined fleets at Aransas Pass and Rockport/Fulton came next—and that included Jackson Seafood.

Then came Port O'Connor and Port Lavaca. In the early days, there weren't many shrimp boats in Palacios, but it developed a pretty good fleet later on. From there, the next significant shrimp fleet docked at Galveston, and there was some shrimping at Port Bolivar and Sabine Pass. Louisiana and the rest of the Gulf Coast had a lot of fleets too.

While I was growing up in Rockport in the 1950s and '60s, I saw our fleet of wooden shrimp boats every day. We owned them, manned them with crews, produced seafood, and ran a shrimp house. I thought of Jackson Seafood Company as a permanent part of the landscape—an enterprise that had always been there and always would be.

We occupied a prime site on the downtown-Rockport boat basin. People called it "The Fish Bowl" because of its round shape. Our magnificent site looked north and east across flats and deep water channels and fishing reefs in Aransas Bay, and all the way to San Jose Island.

Of course I believed that the Fish Bowl had "always been there" too. I could never have imagined, when I was a child, how it and I might change. I could not foresee the later stresses that would bring me into conversation with a man who had helped build that boat basin ten years before I was born.

For the most part, I grew up in a simple world where my father, my uncle, and my grandfather owned and operated Jackson Seafood and related companies. Those businesses not only provided our family's livelihood, but also a secure place of employment for fifty to one hundred men—until the tide turned.

Early in 1970, three pivotal events occurred for our family. First came the death of my grandfather, Stephen Ford Jackson. He was 83 years old and had lived a long, productive life when he died on February 16. But twelve days later, cancer took my Uncle Jim. And he was only 53. Sadly, his eldest son, Jimmy, was getting married in the Philippines on that very day.

Bobby, Norvell, John, Neva, Mary Lucille, and N.F. Jackson

My elder brother, N.F. (Norvell Ford Jackson, Jr.), was in Rhode Island, at the Naval Officer's School, and wasn't informed until after the funerals. I was away at college—Texas A&I University in Kingsville, Texas—but I was able to get home. Along with the other elder grandsons who were there, I served as pall bearer at two funerals in two weeks.

It was tough for everyone in the family, but especially for my dad. All of a sudden, he had lost not only his father and his brother, but also both of his partners in our family business. Daddy got a stress ulcer—right at Uncle Jim's funeral—and had to go to the hospital. Then Grandmother collapsed as well, and was hospitalized in the room next to Daddy.

We had only a short breather before the third terrible thing happened that year: On August 3, 1970, Hurricane Celia smashed into our shoreline. That storm—the most disastrous to hit Rockport since the infamous 1919 hurricane—leveled Jackson Seafood's main facility. I'll tell all about our harrowing storm experience in the chapter titled "Miseries."

For all the rest of that life-changing decade, my father struggled to keep things on an even keel. I hated to see Daddy struggle to run Jackson Seafood all by himself, but I couldn't quit college when I was just a sophomore, planning to become a lawyer.

We moved along. But within a year or so after the deaths in our family, I found myself taking a fresh, hard look at my college curriculum. "What am I thinking?" I wondered. Maybe becoming a lawyer wasn't the best idea for me after all. Daddy didn't press me, but I knew he was hoping I'd come home and help him run the shrimp business.

I had taken the Law School Admission Test and had been admitted to law school, but as I got interested in business, my professors at school—especially Jim McIntyre—encouraged me to turn in that direction.

Part of my change in attitude may have been that the seafood business was looking really good at that time. My dad was making fairly decent money for the first time in his life. Watching that, I began to get excited about the seafood business as a career.

I got a BBA, and then started work on a Master's degree. Right after completing my MBA in 1974, I joined our family business. Daddy paid me $200 a week, and I thought those were big wages.

But by the end of the Seventies, the tide had turned. The decade of the Eighties turned out to be very tough, not only for the seafood industry, but for Texans in oil and gas or real estate as well.

In the midst of that, I had a growing family at home. Debbie Carlisle and I married in 1976, and five years later, Sarah became a part of our lives. Every evening, I came home to the little, innocent face of a sweet baby who knew nothing of the machinations of business. My daughter and the support of my wife got me through the low point of my life. In 1985, Collin joined our family, brightening it as only a little boy can. But it was tough, raising a family and spending too much time away from home, trying to keep our company afloat.

As Jackson Seafood staggered under a combination of dire economic factors, we hit rock-bottom, and finally chose to cease operations. We sold our extraordinary waterfront property in 1990 and our fleet of boats in 1991. The long dream seemed to be over; the swelling tide had ebbed.

I recall the pain of that defining moment every time I look at the framed newspaper page on my office wall. Now, though, the departing shrimp boat buoys me up. It reminds me, each time I face a turning point or difficult decision, that tides do turn, that this, too, shall pass.

Fisheries

Most of the people I work with now would be surprised to learn how much hot, sweaty work I've done—outdoor labor, getting my hands dirty or greasy, wearing jeans with a uniform shirt and white rubber shrimper boots.

When I went to work at Jackson Seafood, my brand new MBA didn't count for much. I did manual labor just like everybody else. Our work day consisted of a series of menial tasks—unloading boats, icing boats, fueling boats, maintaining boats, and moving boats around the dock. My dad, who had graduated from the University of Texas with a Bachelor of Business Administration in Marketing, was even more into our hard labor than I; he was always in the middle of the action.

Basically, our job was to support the work of the shrimp boats. To understand what we did, you need to understand what they did.

Each July, when the Gulf shrimping season opened, Jackson Seafood's boats—like all the others—headed out the passes, into the Gulf. Our boats were designed so that they could stay out there two or three weeks at a time.

When you see a lot of lights in the Gulf at night, that's shrimpers at work, dragging the bottom to catch brown shrimp—the kind that restaurants usually serve. Those shrimp come up off the bottom in the daytime, so we could only catch them at night.

For the most part, by daylight, our shrimpers would be pulling up their net rigs and going to anchor to sleep. Sometimes, though, they'd go on to another spot to be ready to drag the next night.

Many of our captains were Hispanic, and they used a lot of nicknames—Palomito, Tequache, Gordito, Segundo, Flaca. That's how they identified themselves on the radio: "Hey, Palomito!" "¿Ey, Tequache, que pasa?" ("Hey, Possum, what's going on?") They had nicknamed my dad *Toro*, which means "Bull," so they called me *Torito*, "Little Bull." I learned a lot of Tex-Mex from those guys, and they became like family to me.

If you haven't seen a shrimp boat in action, it's hard to understand the function of all the equipment on board. I was in the business for a while before I actually got to go out for a few nights with Captain Tim Benavidez, and that was very enlightening. Once I saw for myself how everything worked, I thought, "Oh, my gosh, that's so obvious now!" And I understood what hard work the crews do; they really earn their pay.

In the early years, we had GM Detroit diesel engines on our boats. We went to a Caterpillar engine, a 343 Cat, in the 1970s, and then to a 3408—a Caterpillar V8-cylinder engine.

Most of our shrimp boats had a big Douglas winch in the amidships area of the deck. Those winches, made in Aransas Pass, were among the best in the world.

Our main winch had two drums, each holding 1200 feet of cable, ⅝- to ¾-inches in diameter. The 1200 feet

of cable on each winch ended with a swivel and a shackle.

From there, bridles led to the shrimp doors (arrow). Each side of the boat held a pair of these shrimp doors, measuring about eight feet by three and a half feet, and made of mahogany or pine. Each door had a steel runner that dragged the bottom of the sea as a 65-70 foot net between the two doors scooped up the shrimp.

But before those rigs went into the water, the crew dropped a much smaller "try" net, attached to a small try-net winch. The crew ran this trial for fifteen

or twenty minutes, then brought the net up to see how many shrimp were in it. That gave an indication of what was down below. If the spot appeared promising, the crew set out their big rigs.

While those nets were down, making a four- to six-hour drag, the crew continued to run the try net, to get a sense of how they were doing. If they weren't catching much in the try net, they might pick up the big nets and move to another spot.

In the late 1970s or early '80s, most shrimpers converted to "four-rigs." Instead of having one big net on each side, they'd have two 35- to 40-foot nets on each side. In order to pull two adjacent nets, though, they needed something in the middle to prevent them from fouling.

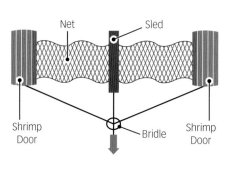

Net   Sled

Shrimp   Bridle   Shrimp
Door   Door

This addition, called a "sled," was an upright piece of steel tied with a shackle to the inside edge of each net. The complete arrangement consisted of a door on the outside, a net attached to it, and to the sled, then the second net tied to the other side of the sled, and to a door beyond that.

In order to pull this contraption through the water, we needed three cables, fashioned into a "bridle"—one cable connected to each door, and one to the sled. The bridle was tied to the main cable, leading to the winch on the boat.

There were lots of lines on a shrimp boat, from quarter-inch to one-inch diameter—"whip lines" to raise and lower nets and hang them up, and polypropylene "lazy lines" to help pull the nets in. Polypropylene can float, and that makes it easier to see in the water. A crewman could simply hook it with a pole and pull it in.

Toward the end of my career in the seafood business, the government mandated that we put turtle excluder devices—TEDs—on our nets. I don't know how many shrimpers ever caught turtles; we very seldom did. But the government considered that if we caught one, it was one too many; we had to stop it altogether.

Shrimpers got very upset over the new law; they worried that turtle excluder devices would prevent shrimp from getting in the big nets, or allow them to escape. It's probably a valid concern, but we were all forced to use the TEDs, and the issue continues in the industry to this day.

After the crew dragged their nets for three to four hours, they brought in their nets, bulging with maybe 2000 pounds of sea life— trash fish, sting rays, and every kind of junk, along with the shrimp. The crew dumped it all on the back of the deck in a mound. Sitting on the deck and using little paddles, they sorted through all that stuff, trying to separate the shrimp from the trash, and shoving the waste overboard. In that 2000 pound load, there might be only 100-200 pounds of shrimp.

Once the crew got all the shrimp separated from the trash, they had to remove the shrimp's heads—"heading the catch," they call it. Bay shrimpers don't usually do that, but Gulf shrimpers do, because they'll be out for a couple of weeks or more. The shrimp keep better when headed, and of course they take up less space.

The crew put the headed shrimp in a basket, washed them down thoroughly, and dipped them in a solution that helped preserve them. Then they put the shrimp in the hold, on ice. The whole process amounted to a lot of work for two or three guys on the back deck.

Most of our boats had some electronics to help navigate and find a catch, but aids like GPS weren't available yet. Typically, we had a CB radio, a VHF radio, and a single sideband. We had Loran A, Loran C, radars, depth finders, and sometimes plotters. That's pretty much all anyone could get at that time.

On shore, a typical day for my dad and me began at Kline's Café (formerly Brocato's), at the northeast corner of Austin and North Streets. That business is closed now, but the building—currently owned and occupied by someone else—still reminds many of us of the Rockport "institution" where people gathered for years.

In the day, that cafe opened at 5:00 or 5:30 every morning, with Daddy and some of his buddies always standing at the door, waiting for Shorty Kline to unlock it. That bunch of guys more or less opened up the place every morning. Daddy always took the morning paper with him—the *Corpus Christi Caller-Times*—and drank coffee while he read it.

When I joined Jackson Seafood after college, I adopted the same habit, but I showed up about thirty minutes after Daddy did. The experience had a lasting effect on me; I'm an early-riser to this day.

I guess it was another sort of "institution" that we always called Jackson Seafood "the fish house," even though we were in the shrimping business. Maybe it was a hold-over from the days before shrimp, when my grandfather and his brother owned Jackson Brothers Company, which only handled fish and oysters.

At Jackson Seafood, we had a secretary and a bookkeeper, and we checked in with them when we left Kline's. But we had very little time to keep track of the business end of things except after hours or on weekends.

We had anywhere from five to ten dock employees, and then we had three or four people on each boat. Add them all up, and we had maybe fifty people working for us. There was the pressure of managing the people, making payroll, paying the bills, and myriad other things to deal with. Keeping track of all that was a challenge, and it seemed like we always had a law suit going on too. Every fleet owner dealt with that, and most of the time the suits were frivolous.

As soon as we saw a boat coming in, presumably loaded up with shrimp, we'd start filling a vat with water. That first step started a long process that began as soon as the boat was tied up at the dock—a routine of "wash 'em down, suck 'em out, count 'em, weigh 'em, put 'em on a truck."

We washed the shrimp down to get the ice off them, and that job could take thirty minutes to an hour. When the ice was all gone, someone would go into the boat's hold with a shrimp rake. He'd rake the shrimp into a trough about 12-14 inches wide, at the end of a suction hose. This big10-inch diameter rigid hose attached to a huge stainless steel tube, like a vacuum cleaner, to suck the shrimp out. The tube ran the whole length of the dock, pulling the shrimp into the vat of water we had readied for them.

As the shrimp sank to the bottom of the vat, they were being washed, clearing away any residue that might be attached to them. Any ice that remained was being melted, too. The shrimp dropped from the vat into a plastic conveyor that led into the fish house.

At the end of unloading, we might have anywhere from three– to four– or maybe ten-thousand pounds of shrimp from one boat. My job was to count them. If I didn't do it, my dad did—we wouldn't depend on anyone else to do that job. The count was very important, because shrimp are bought, sold, and priced according to their size.

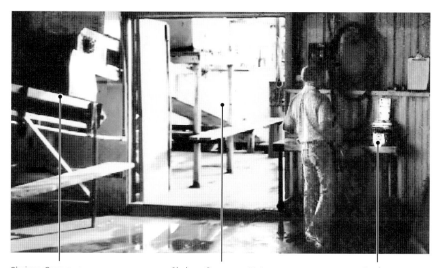

Shrimp Conveyor   Shrimp Conveyor Vat   Scales

As the shrimp came across the conveyor, I took a plastic colander and scooped up about five pounds of shrimp. I dumped them out on a stainless steel table, weighed out five pounds exactly, and counted them by fives to get an average. After I did that enough times, I could identify that bin of shrimp as being, for example, a 26/30 batch—26 to 30 shrimp to a pound.

There was a price for shrimp that size. Another bin might be 31/35's, or it might hold big shrimp—16/20's. I counted each bin separately and wrote down the descriptions, then turned in my tally sheet at the office. The prices changed daily, and the catch was valued on the basis of that price.

A guy stood by our automatic scale, and every time it hit 52.5 pounds, the door opened automatically and the shrimp dropped onto a layer of ice in a wooden box. The employee put another layer of ice on top of the shrimp, then added another load of shrimp, and another layer of ice.

In all, we put 105 pounds in each box, recognizing that about five pounds was water that would drain away. A big shaker jiggled the box to pack it tightly. We pulled the boxes off the conveyor with a big hook, and onto an inclined conveyor that went into a refrigerated truck. Two guys picked up the hundred pound boxes of shrimp and stacked them in the truck. So the whole unloading operation consisted of these five men—the one in the hold, the one at the scale, the one pulling the boxes off the belt, the two in the truck—plus my dad or me.

Each truck headed for the shrimp processing plant as soon as a boat was unloaded and the truck was full. Most of the time, we used processors in Aransas Pass, but we also sold a lot of shrimp up the coast—in Port Lavaca, and sometimes as far away as Galveston. The processors unloaded our hundred-pound boxes, washed the shrimp one more time, sized them, and packed them in five-pound pasteboard boxes. These uniform-grade five-pound boxes were then sold all over the world.

Shrimper crews typically got paid for 35-40 percent of the value of the catch, and the owner kept the rest. But out of his share, an owner would generally pay all the expenses of maintenance, fuel, ice, and so forth. In most cases, crew members only paid for their own groceries and the personal gear that they needed to buy. Sometimes they would pay for other portions of the expense, depending on the deal they had worked out with the owner.

Each time one of our boats came in to the dock, my dad and I wanted to see it unloaded and turned back to the Gulf as quickly as possible. That was our main goal, because the financial ramifications were obvious: a boat at the dock put in fewer fishing days and wasn't making as much money.

While we worked at unloading a boat, the captain and crew prepared to leave it. They were as anxious to stay home for three or four days, as we were to have them get back to work as soon as possible.

The captain always presented a list of maintenance issues—things he needed done on the boat that he ran for us. We'd do everything in our power to get the maintenance done quickly and have the boat ready to go. Then, sometimes, the captain would look for a reason to stay home just one day longer. When the boat just sat at the dock, we'd wonder why we had busted our butts to get the maintenance done.

That created a constant tension for us, because even with that little bit of conflict, we had to be careful. We didn't want to make anybody mad enough to quit. It only happened occasionally, but it was just one more thing to deal with.

Some captains were more responsible than others. Some presented long lists of maintenance needs, but a good captain—one who really took care of his boat—usually had a shorter list.

Captains who had gone home for three or four days preferred not to come down just to move a boat from the fuel dock to the ice dock, or move it over to pull off cables, or to take a boat to and from a shipyard, or whatever. We had to do that job ourselves.

I was eager to move the boats, but my dad was probably a little uncertain, at first, about letting a kid right out of college, with practically no boat handling experience, move a 75-foot, quarter-of-a-million-dollar shrimp boat.

Those boats drew a lot of water—about nine feet, and a foot or two more when fully loaded. There could be other boats around; if I wasn't careful, I might run into one of them. If I got out of the channel, I might run aground or mess up a prop. There could be heavy wind, and our single-screw boats were less maneuverable than boats with twin screws.

I learned how to use a spring-line to get away from the dock. I proved to my dad early on that I could handle the boats, and I became pretty good at it.

Sometimes I'd take a boat to the shipyard, or to Aransas Pass. Going down a channel could be tricky; it might be well marked, or not. Crossing the bay, I might come to a poorly marked section, where I just had to know the way. There were times, even just going from the Rockport jetties out to Marker 49, when a person could have easily gotten into trouble, but I never did.

As we worked through a captain's maintenance list, it might include diesel mechanical issues, or electrical, or plumbing, or welding—almost anything.

We had an all-purpose shop (top of next page) where we did most of that, but we hired specialists in refrigeration and electronics, generally out of Aransas Pass. If any very sophisticated diesel engine work came up, we brought in a B. D. Holt Caterpillar mechanic or maybe an independent mechanic from Aransas Pass or Rockport, who worked on diesel engines.

We didn't do much of the actual engine maintenance—just minor things. We took oil samples and sent them off to a laboratory. Their analysis could tell us if there was a problem with an engine, or what we needed to look out for, so we got

those tests regularly. We changed the oil at the dock, taking extra care to pump it out into a tank; the EPA forbids pumping it into the bay.

Our fish house crew did other kinds of basic maintenance—welding, plumbing, or minor electrical work. There was any number of things that had to be done to keep the boats going.

The bridles to the nets got twisted sometimes. When they got too rusty, we'd have to take them off and put another set of bridles on. Sometimes we had to re-splice the cables or replace the main cable. We were always concerned that we might lose an entire rig, if a cable broke. Each outrigger had stays going forward and aft, and we readjusted those stays with a turnbuckle.

When I had to go down in an engine room on one of the boats, it was really hot and uncomfortable, especially if the engine had been running for a while. There was no ventilation down below the deck.

Working in the ice hold was cool, of course. We'd go there to access the stuffing box, which is the flange and packing where the shaft goes through the hull. Repacking the stuffing box was something we had to do occasionally. If we had a rudder issue, we'd work in the lazarette, at the stern of the boat.

Daddy might be in the middle of all the hot, dirty, smelly work, but if something had to be picked up in Aransas Pass or Corpus Christi, he was usually the one who made the trip. He had the relationships; he knew where to go; he was just good at doing that. He might make a number of stops, getting stuff, while

I stayed at the fish house, doing whatever needed to be done.

Sometimes you might catch me at the end of an outrigger with a cutting rig, trying to loosen up a rusted shackle that wouldn't turn. Or I'd be in there pulling cable off the winch, and getting grease all over my hands, or working in the shop. I just did a lot of manual labor in those days.

My clothes always had a fishy smell; there was simply no way around that odor. I'd leave my jeans in the garage or wherever, and not bring them in the house. My wife, Debbie, got them washed pretty quickly; that was just part of the job.

I didn't always have to do boat maintenance, and wasn't qualified for some of it, but I had to make sure it got done. That's when I became an avid list maker. I'd write down, on an 8x11-inch yellow pad, all the things that needed attention on the boats. I folded a sheet into eight sections and stuck it in the pocket of my shirt—a rudimentary Day-Timer, if you will. When I opened it up, I'd see four or five boat names there, and a list of things that needed to be done. I got in the habit of checking them off every day, and every few minutes I'd ask myself: "What's next?" "What's next?"

I do that to this day, but now I have a small, bound Day-Timer. It's a task-oriented method that I use, to make sure I get things done. I juggle lots of balls every day in my business, so I have to multi-task. Without a list to refer to, it would be very hard for me to keep up. I'm almost a fanatic at list-making, and it started back in the shrimping days.

When we completed our maintenance on a boat, we readied it to go back out into the Gulf. We didn't have freezer boats, but ice boats, so we'd have to send them out with ice in the hold. For years, we bought ice in 300-pound bars and manually ran them through a crusher and blower. Finally, in 1958, we built an ice plant.

This picture (top of next page) shows the interior of the ice vault. My uncle, Jim Jackson, is on the left, and Gene Carter stands beside him in the big concrete block vault. It was maybe thirty feet tall, thirty to forty feet wide, and close to a hundred feet long. When I walked in on the concrete floor of that building, and saw that big mountain of ice in front of me, it was easy to imagine being on a ski slope in Colorado—and on some August days, I wished I was.

Two 671 Detroit diesel engines ran two Frick 9x9 compressors that powered an ammonia ice plant made by the Vogt Company. We sometimes had a refrigeration guy on the payroll, but my dad was always very much involved in that operation. Actually, for many years he *was* the refrigeration guy. He knew enough to run the plant, but it's not something I ever learned nearly as well as he did.

Keeping everything running and maintained at the ice plant was a full-time job. There was always some leak, particularly on the engines; those 671s were known to be bad leakers. So there was always oil around, and soot, and mess like that, from the engine itself. And there were always ammonia leaks. I worked around ammonia my whole life, until we left the business. We were always inhaling it, and some times were worse than others. I don't know what that did to us, healthwise.

Inside each ice-making cylinder were about 150 tubes, each about ten feet long, and about the circumference of a silver dollar. Ice formed around these cylinders, dumped down, and fell in pieces about an inch-and-a-half long. They were cylinder-shaped too, with a hole in the middle maybe the size of a dime.

By the time the ice dropped out of the plant cylinder and onto a screw conveyor, it was in small pieces that continually piled up, making a huge, freezing pile of ice in the vault.

Depending on how hard it was to break up—and how many hands we had available—we'd put three or four guys inside with shovels, and they could literally spend hours in there. Even though it was cool in the vault, that was a tough job.

A couple of guys went up in the mountain of ice, chipping away, and a couple got on the floor, to shovel ice through the steel grate covering our two screw conveyors in the floor. The ice fell through the grate and into the conveyors.

Once, in the late 1950s or early '60s, a guy from Florida came over here to work. His foot slipped through the grate and into the screw conveyor. It cut his foot off. That was a fluke accident which shouldn't have happened, but it did. Of course, after that, we constructed a grate of much finer mesh.

From the two screw conveyors in the vault floor, the ice went onto a single nine-inch diameter galvanized screw conveyor on the dock. It had a cover over it and extended out the dock, starting off at ankle height, and making a gradual incline. By the time it got to the boats lining both sides of the dock, the conveyor was probably eight feet up in the air. There, the ice dropped into a big hopper scale.

Ice was generally sold in 300-pound bars, so, since we were selling it in cylinder form, we set our hopper scale to trip at 300 pounds. It tumbled the ice into a hopper where another screw conveyor moved the ice to a blower. That propelled the ice through a hose and into the boat.

From our home on Magnolia Street, we could tell when the blower was going. It wasn't really noisy enough to bother other people, but we were so sensitive to the sound that we heard it loud and clear. Likewise, if the ice plant shut down, we'd know it also, because we'd notice that the sound had quit.

The job that I usually took was running that ice scale at the end of the dock. I got the conveyor running, stopped it, started it again, made sure it was clear and didn't clog up. If it did jam, we'd have to melt the ice by washing it out, and then restart the blower.

Our fish house provided summer jobs for a lot of teenagers and college kids in this town—probably hundreds of them over the years. And they all had their turn in the ice vault. In the early years, I spent a good deal of time inside with those guys, shoveling ice.

By the late 1970s or early '80s, most people were getting away from all that laborious ice-handling. In 1978, we got on board the movement and installed an automatic ice rake made by Turbo Machinery. The steel rake had huge teeth, like a sprocket, leveling the ice constantly across the entire width of our building.

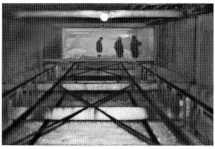

For a sense of scale, note the three people standing in the background of this photo.

Then, instead of ice piling up like a mountain, it all lay uniformly flat.

When we were ready to ice a boat, we could reverse the rake to bring ice back, rather than level it. We only had to open a door, and the ice fell into the conveyor. No one ever had to go inside the vault; everything was done automatically. So for the last twelve years or so that I worked at the fish house, our ice job only required one man on the dock, pushing buttons.

The job of "icing a boat" was one that I did on a regular basis—certainly more often than anyone else. We required the captain to come to his boat for this, and generally we expected him to provide someone to work at the receiving end of the icing process—in the hold of the boat. It would not be unusual for us to put 30,000 pounds of ice—a hundred bars—on one boat, and sometimes a boat took more than that.

Whether shoveled by hand or raked by machine, that ice was really great to take home. In my family, we all grew up chewing ice, and I still chew ice to this day—much to my wife Debbie's dismay!

We had the only ice plant in town, so just about everyone knew about it. People working at various local festivals and school events came in, knowing we'd give them whatever they needed. Some got several ice chests full; others got a truck load. We gave a lot of ice away through the years.

Before our shrimp boats could leave the dock, of course we also had to fuel them. We had a fuel dock on the east end of our property, fed by underground fuel lines.

A big Gulf shrimp boat might need five- to seven-thousand gallons of fuel. That could take an hour, or longer, to load. We had two two-inch fuel hoses, and usually any one of our people could handle both lines. If it was late in the day and nobody was there but my dad and me, we'd do it ourselves.

We put one fuel line on each side of the boat and pumped in the diesel. Obviously, we had to monitor it. We didn't want an overflow, spilling fuel in the water. And we had to keep the boat level. Most of the boats had wing tanks that would

This boat is at the fuel dock. You can see the shop on the left, and the fish house behind it.

hold a lot of fuel, and if we put too much fuel on one side, the boat would list. Some boats had another tank in the bow, in the forepeak.

Some boats also had small tanks in the stern on each side and in the lazarette, but captains generally didn't want to put much fuel there. If the boat was too heavy in the stern, the captain risked running aground, or having the propeller hit something. So we kept most of the fuel amidships and forward in the boat. Keeping everything level was the key.

Fueling was a boring task. I'd just sit there and wait, watching it. I couldn't leave, except maybe for a minute or two, and only if I knew we still had a long way to go before the boat was full.

There were rules and regulations regarding the proper way to fuel boats. Our fueling stations had to be Coast Guard approved, with certain required signage: *No Open Lights. No Smoking.* We couldn't do any welding around there, at least not while we were fueling.

A lot of the captains worked "trip to trip," so some of them, and some of their crews, presented us with money issues. A captain might come in and make a nice, fat paycheck, but then three or four days later, when the boat went out again, his wife would come in and want an advance on the trip just starting out. We became like a second bank for these people—loaning them money, because they didn't manage to save enough between trips.

When we had a good captain, we felt that we ought to help him the best we could, but we tried to control giving advances. There was always a risk in that: What if the trip had to be stopped or cancelled prior to completion? What if an engine blew?

Many times, we advanced money and never saw it again, because the value of the catch was insufficient to cover the crew's groceries which we had to pay for. It's just what we had to do to keep good captains.

Shrimping wasn't our only enterprise. We also had a marine supply store in a 50- by 100-foot building with tall ceilings and a big loading dock. It was more or less a marine hardware store where we sold to the public, along with provisioning our own boats. Juan Rivera ran it for us at first, and then some other people were involved. A good friend of mine, Bill Burton, ran it for about the last seven years.

South of the marine supply store—to the right of it, and hidden in the preceding picture —we had a combination net shop and door shop housed in an old army building. It once might have been a barracks or a mess hall, and it was brought in here by barge, from Palacios, I think.

Net repair—patching holes, or putting on new line—is a true skill. Not just anybody can do that, so typically, we had a net man who handled the job for us.

A tourist looking at shrimp nets would think they are black, but actually the nets are white nylon that has been coated with tar. That keeps them from rotting, and they last longer.

Our net man repaired the nets with white nylon too, and when he finished the repairs, the net had to be re-coated.

He heated tar in a steel vat and dipped the nets in so that the tar would permeate them. After they were thoroughly soaked, he'd spin the tar out in the centrifuge, and then hang the nets on our tall net rack to dry (see page 180).

Nowadays, you see a lot of green nets. They're coated with vinyl, and I think that probably is better. The vinyl doesn't even have to be heated; it goes on almost like paint.

Near our net shop we had a 20,000 gallon overhead fuel tank. In the late 1970s we put in a 100,000-gallon fuel tank that sat on the ground. There was a big retaining wall around it, because if we were to have a spill, we'd have to be able to keep it in from spreading.

In addition to our Gulf shrimping boats, and the few Gulf boats that worked for us, we had ten or twenty bay shrimping boats working for us at one time or another. The majority of Rockport's large bay shrimp fleet, though, worked in and around the Rockport Shrimp Co-Op, or before that, at Johnson Fish Company. It had been on that same site, right across the slip to the south of us.

The bay shrimp industry—fishing for both brown and white shrimp, relatively close to shore—was very seasonal. Those boats started real strong in about mid-May and continued through August or September. It was a very, very intense period—a seven days a week operation.

Fourteen or fifteen boats might show up by 5:30 or 6:00 in the evening, but there was always one we'd have to wait for until 7:30 or so. It was usually someone—a Vietnamese guy, or a local die-hard—who just wanted to get in one last drag. Or a guy had fished in San Antonio Bay, and had a long run back. They had any number of reasons along those lines.

We had to wait at the dock until every one of our boats got in; we couldn't leave, because the captains were expecting to unload their shrimp. Many, many evenings we didn't sit down to supper until 8:30 or 9:00 at night—or later. It seemed we were forever waiting on one last boat.

It was a grind—taking care of our Gulf fleet and the bay boats at the same time. Even though the bay shrimpers did their own maintenance, we had to be there to unload the shrimp, sell the captains some fuel, and give them some ice.

With that intense activity going on, I went seventeen years without a summer vacation. The spring and summer months, when the boats were always out, was when we made our money in the shrimp business. There was no way to leave, never a time when I could really get away. If I did take some time off, it would just be for a weekend. I never had any rest.

Whether we were unloading a boat that had just come in, getting one ready to go back out again, working with the office crew, or managing the supply store, my dad out-worked all of our employees. Everyone—even his enemies—had great respect for him, because of how hard he worked. He took out the trash, he swept the floor; he did it all.

Daddy would go down at all hours of the night to check on the boats and the ice plant. He was the first one at the fish house every day, and the last one to leave every night. That's what he did, so I learned that's what owners are supposed to do. To this day, I continue the habit in my investment practice.

The shrimp industry was thriving in the 1970s, and the Gulf of Mexico shrimp fishery was the most valuable fishery in the United States. The Gulf catch accounted for more than 20% of the total dollar value of fish landed in the United States.

Since Jackson Seafood had such a successful shrimp fleet, we decided to upgrade to steel boats, beginning in about 1971-72. We considered various ship yards up and down the coast, but we were fortunate to have most of our boats built right next door, at RYSCO—Rockport Yacht and Supply Company. We built seven or eight new boats at that time.

Financing was relatively easy. At one time, we could even put about 12½% down, and then take advantage of the Capital Construction Fund. This program, created by the Merchant Marine Act of 1970, was designed to assist U.S. fishermen who face a competitive disadvantage relative to operators in other countries.

The Capital Construction Fund allows fishermen to defer tax on income from the operation of their vessels, and use that money to construct or replace boats as the need arises. The amount accumulated by deferring tax is, in effect, an interest-free loan from the Government.

In addition to the Capital Construction Fund, in the late 1970s there was a 10% investment tax credit. So effectively, we could actually get a boat for about 2½% down. That made it very easy to expand fleets, and a lot of people took advantage of such programs.

Texas' off-season was the best shrimping season in Mexico, so many U.S. boats went there to fish—before its waters were closed to us. The Brownsville/Port Isabel fleets went to Mexico, because they were close by. Folks from Florida shot straight across the Gulf to fish there, too. Shrimpers could spend six months in the Yucatan, or up at Tampico, which was a big place for shrimping too.

We never did go to Mexico, and that may have been just as well in the long run. In 1976, international law established an Exclusive Economic Zone (EEZ), prohibiting any country from fishing within 200 miles of another country's coastline. Mexicans couldn't fish in our waters anymore, and we couldn't fish in theirs.

All the U.S. fleet owners had to stay home, and that put even more pressure on the Texas and Louisiana coasts. Though we didn't recognize it then, that may have been the beginning of the end.

In about 1976-78, some Aransas Pass fleet owners, particularly a family named Duzich, got involved in an East Coast fishery that was new to us: They sent their captains and crews to Virginia to harvest deep sea scallops off the New England coastline, using a dredge.

For that, Duzich constructed boats much larger than those we used in the shrimp industry—maybe 80-90 feet in length, with a beam of 22-24 feet, compared to a shrimper 75 feet long, with a 20-foot beam. That may not sound a whole lot bigger, but the volume is exponential, and that makes a lot of difference. These were really big boats.

The scallop boats were more sophisticated too, with more hydraulics and electronics. They had crew quarters for up to ten or twelve people, instead of the three or four we had aboard a shrimp boat. Of course these larger boats had bigger engines, and they were more expensive. One of them might cost $500,000 to $600,000, while a shrimper ran about $250,000 to $300,000.

But for double the investment of shrimping, a scalloper could expect three or four times the revenue that shrimping would yield. Word travels fast about something like that. Captains and crews in the Rockport area told us a lot about what was going on with Duzich, and the money they were making.

We got the word early enough to take a look at the scallop industry for ourselves. My dad and I went to Virginia and visited Duzich's Aransas Pass-based fleet there. We saw, first hand, how profitable this new fishery could be. It wasn't a matter of "Will we make money?" but "How much money do we want to make?"

Since our shrimp fleet in Texas was making good money, going fine, we asked ourselves, "Why would we want to keep all our eggs in one basket? Let's diversify. Let's build some scallop boats and go out there too."

We thought it would be sort of a hedge, if you will, to be in two different fisheries. Again, relatively easy financing encouraged us as well.

Furthermore, years of experience had shown us that when someone got in financial trouble in a fishery and couldn't make it, there was always a market for his boat in another fishery. Boats like ours can be used in different locales for different fisheries—on the East or West Coast, or Alaska, wherever. We didn't feel that we were going out on a limb at all; we believed that our risk would be minimal.

We contracted to build five new vessels, for roughly $550,000 each. Again, RYSCO built most of them, though we had a couple built at St. Augustine Trawlers, in Florida, too. When we got our scallop boats, they had 3412 Caterpillar engines. We bought lots of those engines through the years—mostly from B. D. Holt, and some from Virginia Tractor Company.

Friends and investors decided to go along with us in the scalloping venture and built eight additional vessels. So there were thirteen boats in all, and we acquired facilities for them at Newport News, Virginia, right on the harbor. (Newport News is in the Hampton Roads/Norfolk area.)

At the time, my brother N.F. (Norvell Ford Jackson, Jr.) was practicing law in Rockport, in partnership with Lola Bonner. But he was having second thoughts about the profession he had chosen. N.F. saw that our new venture would give him the opportunity to join us.

He quit his law practice, moved to Virginia, and became our on-site head of operations. N.F.'s law degree and negotiating skills made him very effective in working with the city and various business people there—Charles Amory, the Fass brothers, and others. A close family friend, Tommy Webb, also asked to move to Virginia to become our "dock captain."

Everyone in Virginia was really excited about all the Texas shrimpers who were coming into their area—Duzich, a couple of years ahead of us, and then us, and then a couple more after us. The first thing you know, there was a lot of capital investment in that community, so the city just opened its arms to us.

In 1979, flush with anticipation of continuing good fortune, Debbie and I moved from our first starter home in Little Bay Shores and built a new, larger home in Harbor Oaks. Too soon, though, everything started to fall apart.

Our new boats took longer to build than we had anticipated, because of their sophisticated hydraulics, and such. They didn't arrive until late in the fall of 1979, so we missed the peak spring and summer scallop seasons. Our first few months were marginal at best. On top of that, interest rates had gone extremely high—and fuel had, too.

My father-in-law, Gerald Carlisle, had invested in one of the boats, naming it *Sue C II*, for his wife. (Earlier, he'd had a Texas shrimp boat named *Sue C*.) Eighty-two days after his scallop boat was delivered, we got word that she was sinking, with nine or ten people on board. And the water was icy cold.

Fortunately, other boats were nearby, so no one stayed in the water dangerously long, and all were rescued safely. But the *Sue C II* went down. My father-in-law's boat! A sense of family responsibility made things pretty tense for me.

It was a full six months before we learned what had actually happened to the *Sue C II*. My brother N.F. met with the insurance adjusters, while he was on Navy reserve duty in Baltimore. He had dressed in his white uniform and ordered a hamburger *tartare*. The blood (apparently) dripped from his chin as he told the adjustors that if they didn't pay the loss, we'd take our annual million dollar premium business elsewhere.

Underwater photographs of the upright wreck showed that its flush-mounted deck plates had leaked. Interviews with crew members revealed that when the boat had pulled in at Newport, Rhode Island, for ice, a crewman put an ice hose through a deck plate, rather than through the center hole, which they should have done. The center hole can be closed from the top, while deck plates are designed to be closed from inside; they couldn't be sealed once the bin was full of ice. The deck plates just sat loosely on the deck, and when the boat returned to sea and took on waves, water seeped through the deck plates, filling the hold. The *Sue C II* had sunk due to laziness and negligence on the part of her crew!

We thought it was the worst possible news at the time—only because we didn't know what was coming. We got through the winter, but when spring arrived at last—the season when we were supposed to catch up—the scallops weren't there.

For some unknown reason, the scallops had practically disappeared overnight. The catch for everyone—all up and down the Eastern Seaboard—was down by about two-thirds. We heard a lot of biological theory explaining that, but for us the story was simple: Our resource had dried up. And on top of that, we had problems with our hydraulics.

Financially, we were *major* behind. The bad winter and worse spring forced us to miss our first quarterly payments to creditors on some of the boats. We tried to stick it out, but by the fall of 1980, the hole had become too deep. We had no assurance we could dig out of it in Virginia.

We decided to take our scallop boats back to Texas, though we knew they couldn't be profitable in the shrimping industry. They cost twice as much, and they used much more fuel than the conventional shrimp boats.

But when we tried to sell our fine new scallop boats, we learned that there was just no demand for them. Fishing boats all across the United States faced the same increased fuel costs that we did; everyone was having a bad year. Our 'ace in the hole' was gone.

Gerald Carlisle, my father-in-law, turned out to be the lucky one. When his *Sue C II* sank, insurance paid for the loss, and he came out whole, giving me some relief for the personal responsibility I felt.

We were aware that countries south of the United States had lower, subsidized fuel costs, cheaper labor, and plentiful shrimp. We hoped that more profitable mix would help us find a home for our boats, somewhere below the border.

In December 1980, my brother N.F. and I headed out on a 17-day trip. We visited the Embassy in Mexico City first. We had planned to go to El Salvador next, but when we got to the airport, we saw guerillas sitting at the bar and decided to skip that destination. We went instead to Honduras—to Tegucigalpa, then on to La Ceiba and Isla Roatan.

From there, we proceeded to Guatemala, Nicaragua, and Panama. I remember staying in a hotel somewhere and having drinks at the bar with someone I suspected of being a Russian spy. I remember machine-gun-toting militia in the streets. That was probably in Managua, Nicaragua; they were probably Sandanistas. We left the airport rather hurriedly.

When we finally got to Cartagena, Colombia, in South America, we found a company, Vikingos, run by English-speaking, U.S.-educated businessmen. The company president, Sr. Espinosa, had guards at his house who carried machine guns too. He delegated day-to-day operations to Sergio Martinez, a U.S.-educated biologist—with a PhD, I think.

Vikingos had a nice facility, and they paid for shrimp in U.S. dollars, based on the New York market. Though Colombia was known as a drug country, this company's people were well above drug-dealing. We felt secure with them. We decided to take our fleet there—not only the five scallop boats, but also our eight shrimping boats—along with our Texas captains.

Thirteen vessels and thirteen captains who had to get passports equaled seemingly endless red tape. But we believed the outcome would be worth the trouble. Most of our captains were Hispanics from Rockport, so their communication with the Colombian crews would not be a problem. Or so we thought.

By late spring in 1981, we had the boats and crews all in place. My brother N.F. moved to Cartagena too, and became bilingual. Although plenty of people spoke English, N.F. knew he could be more effective conversing in Spanish.

N.F. recalls:

Overall, we faced a quagmire of import regulations and graft. It became very apparent early on that getting diesel engine parts into the country was extremely difficult. We'd taken a good amount of engine, electronics, and hydraulic spare parts with us when the fleet moved down. But there would always be something we needed, and arranging to get parts in was a problem. With armed soldiers all around the ports and at the airport in Colombia, we had to take Customs import regulations seriously, if we wanted to function.

Phone service was erratic to non-existent, and there was no internet. I worked a deal with a travel agent to use their teletype and was able to carry on a teletype 'conversation' with Johnny or Gloria Rouquette in the Rockport office.

Every couple of months, I'd fly to Miami on a Friday afternoon. Someone would meet me there with a bunch of parts—Caterpillar rings, pistons, gaskets. I'd stuff them into an extra suitcase, so that I could get the gear in as personal effects, then catch a flight back to Colombia the next day.

There the middle men awaited me—most with their hands out for a bribe to speed the parts through Customs. Usually I only had to pay a $20 'baggage-handling' tip at the baggage claim area.

We had some good help at Vikingos, and we made friends that left a very positive impression. Jaime Delgado, a wiry young fellow, was the classic 'expediter.' His sidekick, Sergio Bezanoff, was the consummate deal maker.

Sergio was a Russian ex-pat, married to the daughter of a former Colombian cabinet minister. Imagine the fun I had conversing with them: Jaime speaking Spanish at teletype speed, Sergio speaking Spanish with a thick Russian accent, and me with fairly elementary Spanish.

I was pretty fluent in conversational Spanish, but coming up with terms like 'power take off,' 'winch,' or 'turnbuckle' was a real challenge. In the evening, I'd look at my version of Johnny's pocket Day-Planner and study how to address the next day's list en Español.

One time, my Spanish wasn't quite good enough to keep me out of trouble. Johnny and I had taken a steady regimen of quinine during our Central and South American expedition, but when I ran out of it I didn't worry about getting more. Well, I caught malaria. For about four days, I was delirious with fever at my downtown apartment. In that delirium, I was unable to pick up the phone and ask for help, because I couldn't figure out how to say what was wrong, or what I needed, in Spanish. Fortunately, the malaria turned out to be a mild case."

You'd think our Spanish-speaking boat captains would have fared better than N.F. did, but their interface with Colombian crews did not go well. Cultural differences were so great that the two groups just could not mix.

And we had engine problems, because Colombia had no restrictions on fuel quality, and did not filter the sulfur from it.

Most of all, the timing of that venture was horrible. The Texas coast hit an all-time record shrimp crop in the summer of 1981—while we had our entire fleet in Colombia! Had we stayed home, we'd have done a lot better than we did in a foreign land. And we'd have saved the expense of getting down there, and getting back.

We stuck it out as long as we could. We'd had the boats in Colombia for less than a year, and had started getting pressure from the scallop boat financial institutions. They didn't like the fact that the boats were operating outside U.S. waters; they were concerned about their collateral. The essence of their multi-page letter to us can be summed up in eight words: "Bring the fleet back to the United States."

We had an inclination to come home anyway, after hearing about the good shrimping in Texas. We repeated our long trip, heading north this time, across the Caribbean and the Gulf of Mexico.

We tied the five big scallop boats to the Rockport dock, and in essence gave them back to the financial institutions. On April Fools' Day, 1982, we went through the agony of filing a bankruptcy petition.

Filing for Chapter XI was a low point for me—and for my dad, too. The event was public knowledge, of course, and that added shame to our agony. Our family had lived in Rockport for so long, and developed such a fine family reputation. Now we felt our honorable legacy falling in shambles. We believed that the stigma would continue forever.

We were proud people, who had been forced into a situation where we had no control and saw no way out. All because of a good idea gone bad.

In many bankruptcies, people are left with practically nothing, but that was not the case for us. What bankruptcy courts are trying to do is put a company back on its feet and give it time to work out its arrangements with creditors. Fortunately, that's the way our procedure worked. The structure of our Chapter XI actually turned into a classic reorganization, as eventually all secured creditors were paid in full.

We didn't want to sell our shrimp boats; we didn't try to sell them. The scallop boats, ninety percent of our debt, sold for twenty to thirty cents on the dollar when they were foreclosed, leaving us with a large debt deficiency. To handle this huge deficiency, we collateralized it by rolling the debt into a note on our valuable Rockport waterfront property.

That allowed us to come out of Chapter XI in 1983, a year after it started, with all secured creditors collateralized. We would spend the next number of years working out an arrangement to liquidate the real estate, which eventually paid all the creditors off. Overall, I take justifiable pride in a Reorganization that progressed in text-book fashion and arrived at a successful conclusion, because all secured creditors got paid in full. I have been learning from that experience ever since, and suspect that I will do so for the rest of my life.

It gave me tenacity, determination, and perseverance.

I held on to my hope and stayed focused.

I believed in myself, my family, and my mission.

I learned that I need never take "no" for an answer, if I thought there might be some way to succeed. ❧

PART II
SHALLOWS

Survival

We still had our shrimp boats working, but shrimping began to die in the 1980s. Everyone in the business spent that decade in Survival Mode. It was a painful experience to try to live through, and shrimping has never come back.

The resource itself was diminishing, and there was more competition for it, especially with the Vietnamese coming in. After the Saigon regime fell in 1975, many Vietnamese refugees found Rockport's climate and geography comfortably similar to their former homes. Many who had been farmers learned how to be fishermen instead.

I have a lot of respect for most of the Vietnamese, because of their work ethic. They worked very hard at shrimping, but many of them openly disobeyed the limit laws. They didn't seem to care initially, but I felt that they should care, because they had become American citizens.

A larger problem for the shrimp industry was lack of support and control over prices, while we struggled to compete in a world market. The entire U.S. fleet, combined, produced only about thirty percent of the total U.S. demand for shrimp at that time, and today our percentage is even smaller. The huge demand was being met by foreign imports from countries that subsidized their shrimping industries—Mexico, parts of South America, Asia.

U.S. shrimpers were not subsidized. Although farmers have always enjoyed subsidies, the shrimp industry never had that benefit. We were trying to compete in a world shrimp market where prices were pretty much dictated by foreign imports. And we had no control over that.

Shrimp boat owners and processors from Texas to Florida organized the National Shrimp Congress, to lobby on the national level. The Texas Shrimp Association worked at the state level. In the photo at top of next page, several of us in the Texas contingent are presenting our case at a hearing hosted by Congressman John Breaux, from Louisiana, one of our main supporters.

Another issue that we faced was lawsuits. The whole maritime legal system falls

Left to right: Sydney Herndon, John Jackson, Bobby Clegg, Congressman John Breaux, Julius Collins, Walter Zimmerman, and Al Silchenstedt

under the Jones Act, which is very different from Worker's Compensation. Plaintiff's attorneys, working on contingent fees, made it easy for crews to make injury claims. Everyone in the shrimp industry had lots of lawsuits going on, because there was a great incentive for lawyers and disgruntled crewmen to team up.

At any given time, our company probably had several pending lawsuits. Ninety percent of them were illegitimate, bogus claims. A shrimper down on his luck would just go find himself a plaintiff's attorney, a well-known lawyer, who knew we had insurance. The crewman would claim injury on one of our boats, even if it never happened, or was exacerbated by something else. Very seldom was there actually a legitimate injury, and if there was, they wanted exorbitant amounts.

Because the claims were more of a nuisance than anything else, insurance companies tended to settle them, rather than fight them. Once in a while we would go to trial, but very seldom. Consequently, our insurance premiums went through the roof. Our annual insurance premium on each boat ranged from about $12,000 to $20,000.

Some of the biggest and most successful fleet owners eventually went out of business. With few exceptions, the traditional fleet owners are gone now.

The people who survived in the shrimping business were mostly those who were the "owner-operators" of their own boats. They didn't have to hire a crew, because they *were* the crew. And of course, when you own something, you take better care of it. Still, very few of the independents are left.

I doubt that Jackson Seafood made a profit in more than two years of the decade of the Eighties. And we still had our huge deficiency as a result of the scallop boats venture. I started getting my grey hair.

Shrimping ceased to be an enjoyable business, and I don't miss it. It was just tough work, seven days a week. I'd always stop and go to church on Sunday, but usually on Sunday afternoon I was back at work.

Even at home, I'd get calls. The phone would ring at 2:00 a.m., and I'd just cringe. No one would be calling at such an hour, unless there was a problem.

I'd answer the phone and hear the U.S. Coast Guard. Or it would be one of our boat captains calling on single side band radio, telling me, "We're taking on water." Or "The engine just blew." Something like that. Then I'd call the Coast Guard, and try to get them to go out there and help. It happened way too often.

Or I'd be down at the fish house, watching the boats coming in from the Lydia Ann Channel. We'd be expecting our boat in, and then I'd see, across the bay, two shrimp boats really close to together, one right behind the other. That meant only one thing: One boat was towing the other. And the one being towed had a blown engine.

Boats heading for the Rockport Harbor turned left, while boats bound for Fulton continued straight ahead. So I'd be waiting to see which way those boats would go. If they turned left, they were our boats, and we were looking at an expense of ten or twenty thousand dollars. Or more. I hated to see that sight. It was like a nightmare.

We had little control over what happened on our boats, once they went off-shore. One thing that happened, perhaps more than we realized, is that a captain would sell some of the shrimp to fishermen, or yachtsmen, out in the Gulf—two hundred pounds here, two hundred pounds there. He'd sell the shrimp for cash, and there would be no way for us to ever know it. The transactions were virtually untraceable. The crew would swear to keep their mouths shut, and hundreds of dollars never made it to our pockets.

Usually we had good crews, but if they weren't around, we had to take whatever men we could find. We were handing over a shrimp boat, worth a quarter of a million dollars, to someone we hoped we could trust—someone to whom, in another situation, we might not even lend a truck.

Once or twice, we found one of our boats abandoned way up the coast, with no shrimp on it. The captain sold our shrimp for cash, and just left the boat there. The loss to us was thousands of dollars.

The oil business was still booming in the early Eighties, and that suggested an opportunity for us. We could convert our scallop boats into off-shore stand-by boats at Gulf drilling rigs. The stand-by boat does nothing but sit there, until someone needs to go get something, or there's an emergency.

Our boats were of a type that could serve in that capacity, but it didn't work out right away. And by the mid-1980s, the oil and gas business had changed; it was undergoing a severe downturn too.

We also tried other fisheries. From about 1984 to 1986, during the winter months, we converted some of our shrimp boats to bottom long-lining. There's a big demand for red snapper and grouper that live at the bottom of the sea.

We took our 5/8-inch cable off the winch and stored it on a spool in the warehouse, then put 1/8- to 3/16-inch cable on each drum. There's a certain kind of a stainless steel snap we put right on the cable at intervals. Tied to each snap was a heavy monofilament leader that went down twenty or thirty feet, or maybe more. At the end of the leader was a hook with bait on it. It was like a trot line in the bay, but much deeper, and much longer—five miles long.

In order to know where our line was, we positioned poles every few hundred feet, going through the center of big red buoys—buoys maybe three and a half to four feet around. A radar reflector topped off each pole so our boat's radar could locate them.

After our line was down for a few hours, we'd pick it up and reel it in. The snapper and grouper were fairly plentiful. We'd catch big ones: fifteen and twenty pound sow snappers, thirty pound groupers—yellow grouper, and some other varieties. Sometimes we caught sharks, too. We'd take the fish off one line, and move on to the next.

We might get back to the dock with five- to seven-thousand pounds of fish. We'd off-load them, weigh them, and put them on a truck; we sold most of our fish by the truckload. We had a few Galveston customers and others in Dallas and New Orleans, but most often, we sold our fish in Florida. We'd ship them all the way over there.

After our big boats were gone, for two years in a row, Daddy and I took our smaller boats to Port Canaveral, Florida during Texas' off-season for shrimp. This day operation seemed a good fit for those boats. We could fish for scallops, as we had in Virginia, but now it would be calico scallops, which were caught with nets instead of dredges.

By comparison to the big-shelled deep-sea scallops with meat the size of a silver dollar, calicos were much smaller—with meat maybe the size of a dime. But in one trip, one of our boats might catch three or four hundred gallons of scallops. Since the meat was very pricey, scalloping was a lucrative enterprise.

We knew that the sharp edges of scallops can cut a net to shreds as it's pulled across the ocean floor, so we planned to take precautions. Our crews would go out with nets similar to a shrimp net, but of heavier mesh, and we added chafing gear to the nets to protect them. When the nets were full of scallops—in thirty minutes to an hour or two of dragging—the crew would haul it in, unload the scallops onto the deck, and drag again.

As the scallops piled up on deck, they'd make mounds six feet high across the entire upper deck. And that would create a problem.

In Texas, we had installed long outriggers on our deep-draft boats to provide stability when the hold was heavy with shrimp. Since the scallops would be on deck, rather than in the hold, they'd make our boats top-heavy, and our long outriggers would be an added detriment, rather than an asset.

To keep our boats from rolling over in the sea off Florida, we'd need shorter outriggers—maybe half the size of those we used in Texas. That meant a major retrofitting of all eight boats: Take the long outriggers off and leave them in Texas. Build new outriggers and new, shorter, galvanized stay-rods. Put them on. Go to Cape Canaveral for three or four months. Bring the boats back to Texas. Take the short outriggers off, and the stays. Put the long outriggers and stays back on. It was a major operation, and quite an ordeal!

Calico scalloping was different from our Atlantic scalloping business. In Florida, we operated out of the Lambert Seafood facility, bought fuel from them, and sold our product to them. We had a little bit of a shop, where we had a welding rig and makeshift-office, and we kept an employee or two there, but we had to do things Lambert's way.

Calico scalloping is a day fishery, and the boats came in every day with their decks loaded with scallops. Lambert had a big 'clam-bucket,' a dredge-like contraption which reached out on the deck, grabbed a batch of the scallops, and put them in a vacuum tube conveyer that went into the plant.

Steam opened the scallops as they went through that big tube. The shells went out one way, through a conveyor, and the meat dropped down into a mesh and went into a processing plant. There, fifty to one hundred people, in a line, cleaned up whatever trash had got through. The scallops then went into gallon buckets to be marketed, but we had no control over the price that the scallops sold for.

Nor did we have much control over the randomly-picked schedule we operated under. Lambert had an around-the-clock schedule, displayed on a big calendar that listed all the boats using their facility. We had to come up to the dock at an appointed time, and we had to be on time. If we were scheduled for 4 a.m., we'd have to meet our boat at the dock at that time.

Typically, our boat would stay at the dock just a while and then go right back out, but the boats were getting beat up a lot because of the nature of the fishery. If we had an engine problem, or a crew problem, or whatever, we'd have to be at the dock to meet the boat and get the work done quickly, so that boat didn't miss its turn in the schedule. If it missed its place in line, we'd have to wait until the next day to go out to sea. That meant losing a day's profits.

Throughout 1987 and 1988, Daddy and I alternated on "scallop duty." I'd be in Florida for a week or two, and then go home to Texas while Daddy worked in Florida for a couple of weeks. We stayed in an inexpensive apartment or motel near the docks, going back and forth at all hours of the night to meet the boats as they came in.

Once during that time, scallops seemed to be more plentiful in the Gulf than in the Atlantic, so the entire Canaveral fleet moved to the west side of Florida. We went with them—our eight boats among maybe two hundred others, working out of a place near Apalachicola, and also out of Port St. Joe, near Panama City.

It was the way we lived, just trying to survive. We even had one boat that went up the east coast for swordfish. It's very dangerous fishing, clearly depicted in the movie, "The Perfect Storm." Those swordfish are a prized delicacy, especially in Japan.

The only difference between sword fishing and bottom long-lining is that instead of having a bottom line cable, as we did for snapper or grouper, we used a floating fiber line that was up to twenty miles long. It floated below the surface, but not on the bottom. When we caught a swordfish, it could weigh five hundred to a thousand pounds.

We could also catch blue fin tuna while swordfishing. Those are like gold. One blue fin tuna could be worth tens of thousands of dollars, especially

Prepping swordfish for air freight shipment.

PVC pipe to circulate sea water on crabs.

A shrimp farm.

on the Japanese market. They're put in a sort of coffin, to protect them from bruising, during shipment on an airplane. Blue fins have to be perfect. This is a real delicacy in Japan. We're talking $15-20 a pound or more.

For a year or so, in Rockport, my friend Bill Burton and I tried the soft-shell crab business. Harvesting those soft shell delicacies was a twenty-four/seven operation, very labor-intensive. Someone had to be there all the time, checking the crabs.

In order to grow larger, a crab must periodically shed its shell—a process known as molting. The shell cracks, and the crab backs out, leaving the exoskeleton behind. The crab's body is very soft then, and it remains soft for about two hours—but no longer. If we weren't watching, we missed those opportunities.

We ran our operation on Austin Street, right next door to the Sea Shell Shoppe, in a building that my dad owned. We built and installed six to ten shallow plywood troughs, each about four feet wide and eight or ten feet long, standing table high. We tied them all together, and rigged PVC pipe to circulate sea water through them. Then we filled the troughs with crabs that we got from local crabbers.

It was an interesting fishery, but we didn't stay in the soft shell crab business for long. We learned that we couldn't generate the necessary product volume or sales volume to make any real money. We looked briefly—but not very seriously—at shrimp farming too.

At the end, after we sold our fleet, we leased out the fish house to a company called Seabrook Seafood. That also turned out to be a less-than-satisfactory situation.

I spent most of the decade of the Eighties struggling to keep afloat in these various fisheries, trying to pull us out of the financial hole that we had fallen into, over about a two-year period in the late Seventies.

At the same time, we were also fighting on another front that was, in some ways, even more challenging: In 1983, our valuable waterfront property had been placed in jeopardy.

Conflict

From: *S. Reese Rozzell, Attorney at Law*
To: *Mr. Norvell Jackson, Sr.*
          Jackson Channel and Dock Company
Date: *August 30, 1983*

Dear Mr. Jackson:

Pursuant to a resolution by the Aransas County Navigation District No. 1, you are hereby notified that you are using and/or occupying [sic] *certain areas along the Rockport Harbor waterfront that is* [sic] *the property of the Aransas County Navigation District No.1, by virtue of Patents No. 16 and No. 125.*

You are hereby requested to contact the Aransas County Navigation District No. 1 within thirty (30) days from the date of this letter for the purpose of entering into a lease agreement with the District for the subject land.

Daddy and I were stunned when this certified letter arrived. It came entirely out of the blue. We had owned and occupied that property for seventy-five years. We had used it as the basis for our Reorganization. All of our debt was collateralized by that unique real estate. We had to take action.

We learned that some of our competitors in the bay shrimp fishery had gotten the ear of one of the Navigation District Commissioners. Through them, the Commission was persuaded to make the claim on our property.

All along the Gulf coast, there has been perennial conflict between the Gulf shrimp fleet (people like Jackson Seafood) and the bay shrimp boat owners, many of which were a part of the Rockport Shrimp Co-op. The bay shrimpers want to catch all they can during a short season.

No one can blame them for that, but Gulf shrimpers took a longer view. We favored conservation-minded techniques for managing the resource. When we went to Austin, lobbying for laws to help us, the bay shrimpers were always there, in the halls of the capitol, fighting us. We were on opposite sides of every issue.

Here's why:

Shrimp are an annual crop, and prolific breeders. In the Gulf, a female of one variety can release five hundred thousand to one million eggs that hatch within twenty-four hours and swim shoreward. By the time the infant shrimp get through one of the passes and into the inland bays, they are one-fifth of an inch long.

These post-larval shrimp continue across the bays to the salt marshes, the small back bays, and the shallow bayous. They grow rapidly, casting off their shells and forming new ones. Of course, the shrimp must avoid predators—trout, redfish and others.

By May and June, tons of shrimp are in the bays, but not in the Gulf. This is the season for the bay shrimping fleet—the boats that everyone sees in the harbors. These smaller operations work the bays by day and come back to the harbor by late afternoon. Most make multiple short tows each day, using small trawls ten to twenty-five feet wide.

The State sets a daily limit for bay shrimpers, but it's not always followed or well-enforced. It was common knowledge that some shrimpers brought in several times their limit each day.

Obviously, any shrimp that is caught in the bay is a shrimp that doesn't get back to the Gulf. Those that successfully elude predators grow to about two inches in length. By about mid-July, they start a long swim back out the passes and into the Gulf, where their reproductive cycle begins again. And that is when the Gulf shrimping season begins again.

Many of our area's bay shrimpers sold their shrimp through The Rockport Shrimp Co-op (see photo at top of next page). It had leased some property from the Southern Pacific Railroad (successor to the old SAAP), and continued to lease it from subsequent owners of the land, including the Jackson Family Trust. Ironically, our competitors had become tenants of our family trust. And they must have felt vulnerable.

My dad contacted the law firm of Kleberg, Dyer, Redford & Weil, in Corpus Christi. Our family had been with that firm since 1935, and we were one of their longest-running clients. Dad's college buddy, Harvey Weil, had become a well-respected attorney and a partner in that firm. He had written much of the existing State law regarding navigation districts and he represented the Port of Corpus Christi.

Now we asked him to represent Jackson Seafood and our Family Trust, to remove the cloud placed on our titles by the Aransas County Navigation District.

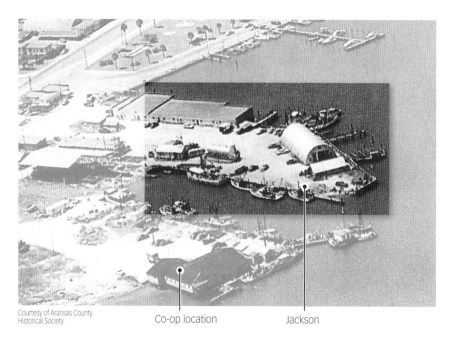

Courtesy of Aransas County
Historical Society   Co-op location   Jackson

Jackson Seafood and the Family Trust were separate entities which held separate parcels involved in the claim. I was not a beneficiary of the Trust. Each parcel had specific merits and arguments in its favor, so Weil advised that each entity should seek separate legal counsel.

The Trust then hired Judge Allen Wood, a retired judge, who was still practicing law with the Wood & Burney firm. We had a team of two great attorneys—and significant legal expense.

To save money, I offered to become the paralegal for both attorneys. For the next three years, I found myself heavily involved in the discovery phase of our suits—researching documents at the courthouse and in our files, finding surveyors' records, locating deeds, reading court records and depositions and Navigation District minutes. I spent hours, every week, on this sort of thing, in addition to helping run our seafood business. I could probably write an entire book on the intricacies and details of this litigation alone.

What I knew, and what I learned, combined to make this complete picture: In the 1880s—about the time that my father's grandparents, Elisha and Irene Barton Norvell, were getting settled in Rockport—the SAAP Railroad had a rail line that came through downtown Rockport. It crossed Austin Street just south of the Shell Shop, then ran several hundred feet into the bay, just north of, and contiguous to the Rocky Point for which the City of Rockport was so aptly named.

Rail cars did not go out over the water, but stopped at the shoreline. Beyond that point, push carts moved along the rails. Boats waited at the end of the line for those push carts to off-load the fish, oysters and crabs they had brought in.

As Rockport developed, that rail line became the dividing line between the original Smith and Wood Subdivision survey of Rockport, and the newer Doughty and Mathis Subdivision.

By 1930, the rail was not used anymore. My dad's father, Stephen Ford Jackson, bought the railroad pier and leased some adjoining land from SAAP. They didn't charge much for their leases, since they weren't using the property.

Jackson Island   Fulton/ Bruhl   Hoopes/ Smith

Courtesy of Aransas County Historical Society

In 1935, my grandfather, Stephen Ford Jackson, formed Jackson Channel and Dock Company, Inc. as a land-holding company, conveying to it the bay front property that he already owned. It was a shell corporation that owned the land, and it was the first corporation we had. (Jackson Marine Services, Inc. followed in 1957, because we got into the ice, fuel, and boat repair business. The seafood business was not a corporation, but simply a partnership originally; we incorporated it later as well.)

Since Jackson Channel and Dock pre-dated the State's patent to the Navigation District, our corporation originally had the right to engage in activities that later became the right of a navigation district. We could dredge channels and build harbors, under a charter to Jackson Channel and Dock Company, Inc.

When the Aransas County Navigation District formed in 1925, they were to build their harbors, and their jetties, and that sort of thing, on submerged lands east of the shoreline, following the meandering shore. The next year, they set to work, creating a rudimentary harbor behind an uncapped rock jetty. That early harbor lay south of the downtown area where the Fish Bowl Harbor would be situated in 1940. The ACND's dredging created spoil south of Jackson Seafood, toward the Westergard Shipyard (property that would become Rice, and then RYSCO).

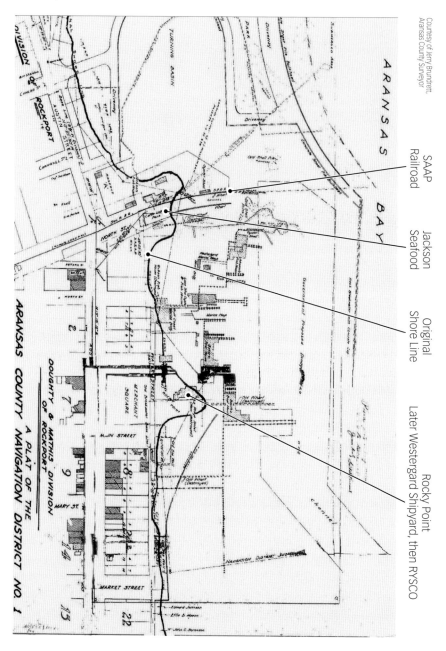

Courtesy of Jerry Brundrett, Aransas County Surveyor

SAAP Railroad

Jackson Seafood

Original Shore Line

Rocky Point Later Westergard Shipyard, then RYSCO

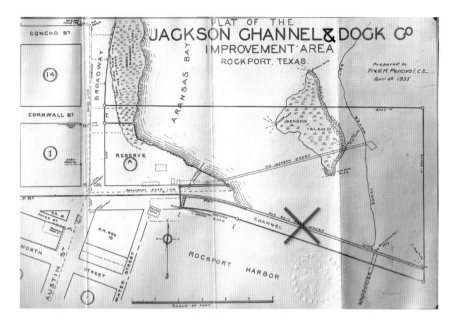

Plat of the Jackson Channel & Dock Co Improvement Area, Rockport, Texas. Prepared by Fred M. Percival, C.E. April 4th 1935.

In 1936, the State issued to the Navigation District a patent (in essence a deed) that defined and conveyed to them their submerged property holdings and responsibility. Then, some of the things that Jackson Channel and Dock had been able to do were taken away from us.

A few years later, the Aransas County Navigation District wanted to extend the harbor to where it is now. For my father and grandfather, that proposal represented a radical change. Part of the Rocky Point, source of our town's name, would have to be blasted away to make the harbor's entry; the old railroad pier that my grandfather owned would have to be cut through the middle.

My grandfather and my father walked out on that pier, accompanied by an impressive group: the three Aransas County Navigation District Commissioners (A.C. Glass, D. M. Picton, and Travis Bailey), Bill Bauer of Bauer-Smith Dredging Company in Port Lavaca (who had the dredging contract with the Aransas County Navigation District), and County Surveyor Floyd G. Huffman. Someone painted a big red X on the pier, where it would have to be cut.

"Fine," my grandfather said, "but . . ." He agreed to the cut, without cost, in exchange for *allowing the dredged spoil to be deposited on the upland Jackson property*. Further, my grandfather required that *the property line between Jackson and the submerged harbor would be determined accordingly*.

Although this agreement was as significant to my grandfather then, as it was to us much later, the deal was made on a handshake. In those days, a man's word was his bond.

The Aransas County Navigation District (ACND) began capping and extending the old rock jetty in 1939. Then they started work on what would become the Fish Bowl Harbor.

Over the ensuing years, my dad became good friends with the railroad's land man, who came down from San Antonio about once a year. The land man just wanted to check in, and to look at the parcel of land that the railroad still owned, adjacent to our property (see preceding plat).

My dad had always told him, "If y'all ever decide you don't want this land, or don't need it, if it's surplus, or what have you, let us know. We'd like to buy the portion we're leasing from you."

And that's exactly what happened in 1982, when the land finally became available for sale. Ironically, we were not in a position, financially, to purchase it at that time. Another local man saw it as an investment and bought the land, but we were fortunate to be able to acquire it from him later on through our Family Trust. That four or five acres lay immediately south of Jackson Seafood, between us and our "next door neighbor," RYSCO.

That property, combined with ours, totaled about seven acres of land—part of the acreage that the Navigation District was now claiming.

The basis of the Aransas County Navigation District's assertion was their interpretation of State Patent law. The ACND believed that all the land east of the *original* patent line belonged to them, not to us.

We contended that ACND dredging had created spoil on our site and all along the waterfront, extending our land further eastward and northward, according to the agreement made with my grandfather in the late 1930s.

We based the Trust Property case on two main principles. First, a statute of limitations had passed. The ACND had waited almost fifty years before asserting its claim. Secondly, we had in our favor the legal principle of adverse possession without any challenge for a very long time. There was much more, but these points were really the core of our Trust case.

The Jackson Seafood portion of the property (the northern portion) had the same statute of limitations and adverse possession arguments. It also had the benefit of an even stronger argument—my grandfather's agreement with the Aransas County Navigation District when he consented to let them cut the railroad pier. Although we never found any written contract of that agreement, we could prove it existed in a court of law.

County Surveyor Floyd Huffman had commemorated the agreement in a certified survey plat showing the new property lines. It was filed of record in the County Courthouse. That plat and the sworn testimony of my dad were valuable information, but we also needed the testimony of a disinterested third party—the dredger, Bill Bauer.

Harvey Weil and I drove up to Bauer's ranch at LaWard, to take his deposition. It was amazing to listen to this seventy-seven year old man corroborate the story exactly as my dad (twenty-four or twenty-five years old at the time of the event) had remembered it.

Mr. Bauer gave me an aerial photo of the harbor, in color, taken in early 1940, right after the harbor dredging and wood bulk-heading had been completed. It was to become our Exhibit A in the trial, and now, framed, the photo hangs on my office wall. There's a copy of it in the Album section of this book.

Here's some of the flavor of Bill Bauer's deposition, which we took in preparation for trial:

> **WEIL:** *You said your dredge lay there and Mr. Huffman told you that you couldn't begin removing the wharf. . .*
>
> **BAUER:** *Yes, sir. It become [sic] quite a problem. We couldn't afford to lay there very long. So finally there was a meeting called of the members of the Navigation District. Those present were Mr. S. F. Jackson, his boy Norvell, Floyd Huffman, A. C. Glass (we used to call him Pop Glass), and Captain Bailey and myself. We all met on the wharf over here and tried to resolve the problem of us cutting this wharf, and the Navigation District reached some agreement with Mr. Jackson whereby we could go ahead and remove this structure and get to dredging, just go right ahead. . . .*
>
> *I remember very well Mr. Jackson stating to us and to Mr. Huffman and to Captain Bailey, who seemed to lead the negotiations, was that the Navigation District, if they would agree to have Mr. Huffman go ahead and survey certain land down in here which he was to receive for the cutting of that wharf, we could then proceed.*

Reese Rozzell followed Mr. Weil's questions with his own, and then Mr. Weil questioned Mr. Bauer further, holding the photograph Bauer had given us.

> **WEIL:** *Does the area of the Rockport waterfront which runs southward from the slip which you mentioned dredge out as shown in this photograph, were any changes made in that or does that photograph depict it as it existed prior to the time you came in to do the dredging?*
>
> **BAUER:** *Just when we took this photograph, that's the way it looked like and that's the way I remember it so very well, and I remember it ever since the 1915 hurricane when we landed about 100 miles down here and*

I am trying to think of the tug's name that was ashore, and Mr. Herring met us down there and we delivered 5000 loaves of bread. My father and me [sic] were there since 1915, and I remember the waterfront of the Rockport area.

WEIL: *But said another way, then, in looking at the photograph which will be marked as Plaintiff's Exhibit 1, is it fair to say that none of the work you did affected the waterfront south of the slip?*

BAUER: *None whatsoever.*

WEIL: *And that depicts it as it existed prior to the time your work began.*

BAUER: *Yes, sir.*

Bauer's sworn testimony, along with my dad's, and Huffman's plat, proved that there had been a valid agreement. With all of this, and much more in our favor, it just did not make much sense to go to the expense and the time required to go to trial.

Still, Harvey Weil convinced us that we needed to give something to the Aransas County Navigation District—I'd call it "a log to walk out on." The ACND commissioners were out in front of the public, and shouldn't appear to just "give in" to us. Mr. Weil came up with a brilliant solution, giving both us, and ACND, what we were looking for. It was a plan that Weil had previously used in Corpus Christi, to good effect.

By this time, I had an ally or two in the Aransas County Navigation District. Utilizing a provision allowed for real estate conflicts, I persuaded the Commissioners to let me come to them in closed session (without attorneys in attendance) to present our case.

I spent several days organizing our documents, plats, deeds, and photos in chronological order. They provided a complete historical account, easy to follow, beginning with the original deed dated 1906, and including a State charter that showed Jackson Channel and Dock, my family's company, owning some of this property.

On the night we'd agreed to meet, I sat down before the commissioners (increased in number from the early days and now a group of five). For three hours I explained our position. Once I laid out our case and convinced them they were likely to lose the law suit, I showed them the log to walk out on:

What they were looking for was additional revenue for the District—a lease on the property. We were looking for a clear title to our property. We proposed that if they would give us a fee simple clear title (which we would have gotten if we won), we would agree to pay them a "waterfront access user fee" based upon X dollars per lineal foot of bulkhead. This would be similar to the funds they would have gotten in a lease, had they prevailed in the lawsuit. Both sides would win.

The Navigation District Commissioners went for it. We cut the deal and put it in writing. Then it had to be approved by the Texas School Land Board, as are all agreements dealing with land that had originally belonged to the State. Part of the teachers' pension program is based on the land that the State owns. Actual approval by the School Land Board did not come until 1986.

I got me one hell of an education over those three years. To this day, I feel that I know more about the Aransas County Navigation District and waterfront history than anyone else in Aransas County. We had a lot at stake. I had to become an expert on all of that, in order for my family to survive.

The Waterfront

By the mid-1980s, it became apparent to me that we Jacksons wouldn't have a long term future in the seafood business. But what in the world could I do, to get out of it? No one wanted our boats; everyone had the same problems we did.

Incredibly, there was no market for the extraordinary property we had to sell: Waterfront property on a deep water channel. Property that writer William Allen termed "beguiling" and "one of the nation's special sanctuaries." He compared Rockport to Taos, Big Sur, Aspen, and Key West.

I felt confident that our property was the most valuable thing that we had— if we could figure out some way to use it.

I started learning about waterfront development. I attended a couple of waterfront development conferences on the East Coast, and I got some help from developers in our area, particularly in Corpus Christi.

I began to put together a visual plan of how our waterfront could become a mixed-use waterfront retail and residential complex. But the seven acres belonging to the Jackson Trust and to Jackson Seafood properties really didn't seem like enough. And anyway, who would want to put in a nice development, next to a dilapidated shipyard?

RYSCO, our next door neighbor, was a family-owned company, just as we were. And the Smith family, like the Jacksons, was having its problems.

RYSCO had no one to build boats for. OPEC-influenced high oil prices in the 1970s had created an oil glut in the 1980s. Reduced demand and overproduction then caused oil prices to drop; in 1986, they dropped by a whopping 46 percent. The world price of oil, which in 1980 had peaked at over $35 per barrel in the U.S., fell in 1986 from $27 to below $10. Oil companies that had been RYSCO's good customers no longer had any need for new oil field supply boats.

To make matters even worse, RYSCO was part of the Smith family's parent company, Luling Oil and Gas. That company was in dire straits—probably even worse than Jackson Seafood was. They were pretty much out of business.

So, with a lawyer's help, I approached Tommy Smith and Sam Simpson, of RYSCO, and we got their property under contract. With that, I was able to acquire the rights to the RYSCO property—about nine acres, including what they owned and leased. Combined, we had about sixteen acres in downtown Rockport, with 3200 lineal feet of waterfront.

A modern photograph hardly suggests what historic land this is: In 1845 Zachary Taylor put his troops ashore right here, on the rocky point of land later blasted away to build the Fish Bowl harbor. The La Playa Hotel, built on that point in 1900, offered refuge to a few frightened souls during the awful 1919 Hurricane.

The Del Mar Hotel once stood nearby, at Merchant Square. It was extraordinary in its time, luring weekend visitors from San Antonio and elsewhere. The Bailey Pavilion (see top of page 83), extended out into the bay from this shore, as did working piers and docks.

The property is unique, as well as historic. Imagine driving the coastline, starting at Brownsville and continuing all the way to Key West. Where do you see anything like what we have here? Not in Florida, Alabama, Mississippi, or Louisiana. And nowhere else on the Texas Gulf Coast.

This perfect combination exists only at Rockport, Texas: a deep-water port in a downtown setting, within walking distance of shops, art galleries, museums, beaches, and hundred-year-old homes shaded by windswept live oaks. Property at the edge of a wildlife sanctuary protecting pelicans, herons, cranes, roseate spoonbills, skimmers, seagulls and migrating birds.

I tried for several months, in the late Eighties, to find an investor for this property, or someone to help put a deal together. But in those years, if you had money, you didn't put it into real estate, and if you'd been in real estate before, you were broke.

I went to a local banker and asked him what I could do with my unique

The
La Playa
Hotel

The
Del Mar Hotel/
Aransas Hotel

acreage. He suggested that I give Mr. Perry Bass a call.

"I don't know Mr. Bass very well," I said. "Would you call him for me?"

"No," the banker replied. "You call him."

What I *did* know about Perry Bass was that he symbolized wealth and oil in Texas. He had learned the oil business at the elbow of his uncle, Sid Richardson, who willed him about $11 million in oil properties and real estate.

Mr. Bass had set up Bass Brothers Enterprises in 1960, to manage the family's enormous oil and ranching interests. No one really knew the extent of the Bass fortune, until Mr. Bass became chairman of the Texas State Parks and Wildlife Commission. He was then required to file a financial disclosure statement, and it showed that the family owned a large part of downtown Fort Worth and collected royalties from sixty-eight oil companies in twelve states.

I knew a few other things, more personal things, too: That Perry Bass and his wife Nancy Lee were private people, modest people. They enjoyed nothing more than quiet time at their San Jose Island ranch house. Bass himself had designed and built that house in 1937, for his uncle. Mr. Bass knew my parents by first name; he knew the whole family. He had promised, at the time of our Aransas County Navigation District lawsuit, to give a deposition about the cattle pens he kept on the RYSCO property, to serve his ranch.

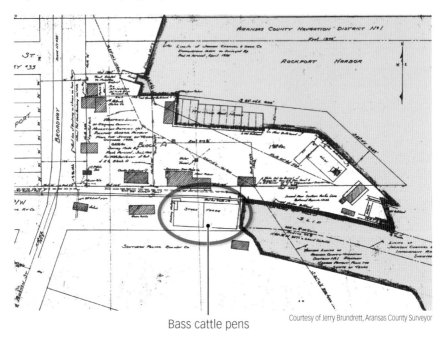

Bass cattle pens

I felt confident that contacting Mr. Bass would not be a difficult thing to do. When I dialed his phone number one day in 1989, he accepted my call.

"Mr. Bass, this is Johnny Jackson. How are you, sir?"

"Fine, Johnny. How are your mom and dad?"

"Oh, they're fine."

And then I said, "Mr. Bass, I'm calling to talk to you about this property we have. You know it very well. You've known it for years, and you love Rockport. I've put together a real estate development deal on it, as well as the property next door. Would you have any interest in looking at it?"

"Yeah," he said. "I think I would. Just send it over and let me take a look at it." So I had the proposal delivered to him.

About two weeks later, Mr. Bass sent his real estate guy from Fort Worth. We spent one afternoon walking the property, visualizing, talking about it, going out on the jetties to look at it from that side. Then we went to another office in town and literally struck a deal on a napkin—a classic, back-of-a-napkin type deal.

Working out the details came later, and that was very intricate. We spent a year getting all that done. One of Harvey Weil's partners, John Brooke, was the real estate attorney who helped me with that. And I guess there was a whole team of Bass lawyers. But the whole concept pretty much started that one afternoon, when we walked the property and scribbled on a napkin.

We negotiated a deal, and I thought it was fair, because we were just a small town seafood company, trying to survive up against Billionaire Bass. They're tough, tough negotiators, and they didn't give anything away. Yet they treated us fairly, and I've never forgotten that. On October 2, 1990, after a year of putting the deal together, we closed the transaction with Rockport Harborfront, L.P., a partnership controlled by the Bass family.

In essence, that sale paid all of our debt. We didn't take any money away from the table—maybe a little bit here and there, but hardly anything. We literally got out of it with the shirts on our backs. But we were able to pay off the scallop boat debt and everything that we'd accumulated. This sale to Perry Bass freed us up, gave us the ability to start over.

I was forty at the time, and I'd lived through all those years of shrimp industry problems, and the scallops, and the law suit—all that stuff. Well, they say life begins at forty, and here I was, looking to start a second career.

I couldn't imagine not being involved in Mr. Bass' development of the land that my family held for so long. I wanted to be a part of it, and they agreed to hire me as property manager. I got my real estate license in 1990. We had many important things to accomplish—demolition and removal of buildings and cleaning up after them; attending to environmental clean-up, like the removal of underground storage tanks; negotiating leases with some of the Austin Street tenants.

While I was working for Bass, my dad was still running the shrimp fleet. I helped him, too; I was doing both jobs. We spent a year or so tearing down old buildings at RYSCO, for salvage. Then we got to a point where we leased out our shrimp house. And all this time, we were still trying to figure out how to get rid of the shrimp boats.

I'd hit a home run with Bass, but we still had those boats that we couldn't even give away. Little did I know that I could achieve a second impossible thing in the 1990-91 period. Two home runs, two impossibles, back to back.

This story began, in a way, in 1982, when Miguel de la Madrid was elected President of Mexico. He promptly nationalized all the private-sector businesses in Mexico, including shrimp fleets. Fleets that had operated like ours, family-owned, were taken over by the government during de la Madrid's tenure. Of course that was a miserable failure—the government never gets anything right. The boats turned into rust buckets, because no one did any maintenance on them.

When President de la Madrid's term expired in 1988, the people of Mexico replaced him with Carlos Salinas de Gortari. He was a significantly younger man, U.S.-educated, holding a Harvard MBA. He spoke fluent English and had a free-enterprise philosophy. He reversed de la Madrid's laws and re-privatized Mexican industry.

I heard about this through my shrimping-industry buddies in the Port Isabel/ Brownsville area. They were leaders in the shrimping industry. We'd fought 'wars' together, going to the State and Federal capitols to plead our case in fisheries legislation, during the years I had served on the board of the Texas Shrimp Association. And many of them had connections in Mexico.

All of a sudden, there was a demand for used shrimp boats, and my buddies knew about it, early on. They put me in touch with the Ramirez family in Ciudad del Carmen, who had run a family-operated shrimp fleet off the Yucatan Peninsula. Now this group was trying to get back in the business that de la Madrid's presidency had taken from them.

In 1990, they agreed to purchase our six steel boats (our two wood boats were sold to a man in Palacios), but it took until May of 1991 to close the deal. The Ramirez family had all the support they needed, the backing of influential politicians, but still the red tape, dealing with the Mexican government, was *unbelievable*. Take what we have, multiply it by ten, and you've got Mexico.

One day in May, the day depicted in the newspaper article framed on my wall, our steel boats rounded the jetty, heading for Mexico. That was the End of an Era, when our boats sailed away. . .

I have never seen them since that day, but our boats probably still exist. I'll bet they're still there.

A Wider View

And what about RYSCO, who got the same letter from the Navigation District that we did? Well, the Smith family, who owned RYSCO, didn't have the same history and merits to their case. Acting on behalf of his family, Tommy Smith acquiesced and signed a long-term lease. I think he acted too quickly, but he did what he thought was best. The family was involved in other businesses; they didn't want to be interrupted by litigation.

We felt that we had every reason to fight the Aransas County Navigation District ruling. But somehow, in some people's minds, our decision in contrast to that of the Smiths, made us out to be the villains. In later years, their decision left a jumble of leases and ownership, with no clear understanding of what was RYSCO's, and what belonged to the ACND or other interests.

The current owners have a discombobulated mess, without a lot of contiguous fee-simple property. The middle of the property is fee-simple, but at both ends, there's some Navigation District property. That makes it very difficult, for land-use planning.

Long story short: The Basses hope to do a land swap with the Aransas County Navigation District, so that all their fee simple land will be contiguous.

I've asked Tommy Smith to share his experiences from this difficult period that we went through.

Tommy Smith Remembers

I've always been called Tommy, but my full name is Thomas Noah Smith III. My father, T. Noah Smith, Jr., went by the nickname "Tiny."

My grandfather, the original T. Noah Smith, grew up in San Angelo, but somehow or another, he ended up in Aransas Pass. He watched old Conn Brown sailing around in a little sailboat, and was so jealous that he rustled up some packing crates to build a sailboat for himself. He decided that if he ever had any money, he'd come back to this area and live, or have a home down here, on the water.

I guess he moved to San Antonio in about the 1920s. He had a restaurant on the San Antonio River, and while he was there, he met an oil promoter named Dr. Sutton. Sutton walked in and showed my grandfather a core, or something, from Luling, Texas. My grandfather put together some money from various investors and went over there to drill a well. It turned out to be the discovery well of the Salt Flat Field, which became Luling Oil and Gas.

My grandfather had a fifth grade education, and he found that oil with a doodle-bug—a dowser-like contraption. He hired a geologist—probably the brightest one he ever had—but that guy just didn't have enough tact. He told my grandfather that his doodle-bug was nonsense. Well, it was nonsense, of course, but he shouldn't have said that to his boss!

When my dad went to work with my grandfather, his first assigned chore was to fire that geologist. T. Noah Smith was beginning a remarkable career as an oil man, with wood derricks and steam rigs. He worried about moving his drilling rigs to East Texas, but ended up with a couple of leases there that were just unbelievable. That was just the most amazing oilfield in the world.

My grandmother loved antiques, and my grandfather loved Rockport. He wanted a summer house there, so, even though he hated old stuff, he bought his wife the historic Hoopes house at 417 Broadway (Hwy.35 Business). That was in the 1930s, and one of Hoopes' heirs still lived in the back upstairs bedroom; the place was a mess. But it had an eight-foot elevation, and had never had water in it from a hurricane. My grandfather dedicated the next several years and thousands of dollars in restoring the house to its former grandeur. It has remained safe from rising water in any storm since then.

We enjoyed many family vacations in that big yellow house overlooking the bay. My mother and the kids stayed all summer. My dad had an old Twin Beach airplane that he got at surplus, or something, so he'd fly to the Aransas County Airport on Thursday afternoons and fly back to San Antonio on Monday. (Dad flew his own planes until about the time I started flying. He had a heart attack and didn't want to renew his license after that, so when I was flying, he'd just get in the back and go to sleep.)

I went all through school in San Antonio—TMI for high school, and then I graduated from Trinity University. A few years later, I was married, with a little boy of my own to take to the summer house in Rockport.

At the same time my grandfather bought the Hoopes house, he had purchased some property just south of Rice Shipyard—land that included the remains of the Rocky Point that had given Rockport its name. My grandfather started a small boathouse and repair business there, naming it the Rockport Yacht and Supply Company.

North of the Rice Shipyard, on a narrow strip of land between it and Jackson Seafood, were Gibson's Oyster House and Johnson Fish Company. The land extended east farther than it does now. It had built up from oyster shells that Johnson deposited there. The Navigation District did some maintenance dredging later, and probably took the shell point out then. Jimmy Sorenson worked at Johnson's for a while, I believe, before he got his bank job; he was Johnson's accountant, or something.

The Jacksons and Johnsons were neighbors there for years and years, and also lived right across from each other on Magnolia St. Travis Johnson, Jr. ("T.J.") lived a few blocks away, and later had several boats that worked out of Jackson's fish house. He's one of those guys who would drive around in his pickup and manage his boats that way. He didn't get too active in the physical side of the business, but he was in the field daily.

The Jacksons were our neighbors too—on the harbor front, and also in the shrimp business and in the scallop business. We went through some of the same heartaches.

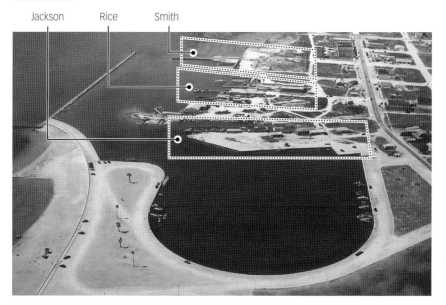

Jackson   Rice   Smith

My grandfather bought a dredge and got a guy to come work on his property. He filled in the land, using the dredged sand, and put in a bulkhead. Grandfather thought it was such a neat idea that he could make land.

He built a pier then, too, and it was really a fantastic thing for keeping the water calm. He rented boat slips to some people, and he had two boat houses. One sheltered his 45' boat, *Lady Cora*, named for his wife, my grandmother. The longer boat house held *Adroit*, his 104' wooden boat—a huge boat for its time.

On December 7, 1941, Japan bombed Pearl Harbor. Three days later, the U.S. Navy commandeered both of my grandfather's boats, the *Adroit* and the *Lady Cora*, for use as submarine patrol boats off the Texas coast. He gave them to the military proudly, feeling so patriotic to let them use his personal boats.

We actually did have enemy submarines in the Gulf, off Port Aransas. I heard a story about a U-boat that had come in through the jetties, but I guess that was just local legend. Apparently, what really happened was that a 400' Liberty cargo ship, the *Worthington*, was torpedoed off the Yucatan Peninsula and towed through the Aransas pass. It sank at the west shoreline of San José, just opposite the lighthouse. Later on, we liked to tie up to it and climb onto the superstructure to fish.

Lighthouse ⌐ ⌐ Mud Island

After the war, the Navy had no further use for my grandfather's two boats, *Lady Cora* and *Adroit*. Someone called with a curt message: "You come get these boats within a week, or we'll blow them up." My grandfather was so disappointed in their attitude, and even more so when he saw that those boats, of which he was so proud, were all torn up.

About once a year, my grandfather had to take his boats over to Rice's to haul them out. It wasn't always a pleasant experience. My grandfather was a volatile old guy; he and Rob Roy Rice were two old coots who just didn't get along. So, in the late 1940s or early '50s, my grandfather decided to build a facility to haul his own boats out.

He talked to a machinist, Jack Williams, in his oil company in Luling, Texas. We had our own drilling rigs and equipment, so Jack ran a fantastic shop to maintain all that stuff. He was a graduate of Purdue University, well qualified to design the haul-out lift and all the rails. When he got it all made, he brought everything down to Rockport and installed it. That was probably one of the first horizontal lifts—elevator lifts—ever built. It was really neat, and it was built out of oilfield gear boxes and drums.

It was probably the only lift in the world like that, until Pearson invented what they call the sinker lift. It was like a flat platform that went down into the water. When a boat came up, they could move the chocks up against the hull, and then the whole lift rose out of the water. The entire section between the piers was out over the water, and it worked like an elevator, submerging to allow a boat to enter the slip for haul-outs.

Piers

Chocks

Courtesy of Tommy Smith

From the lift, we put the boats on dollies that rolled around on cars, and they could go all over the yard. They had a roundtable that could switch them into different spots. In the day, that was the modern deal. Later on, the travel lift was even better.

Eventually, the *Adroit* got dry rot, and my grandfather was so disappointed! He built a big shed there, and kept the boat in it for twenty years. Then we demolished the boat and moved the building before we built the big shed.

We didn't tear the boathouses down until after we were building boats in the 1960s. We built our big shed, and started laying boats on the bulkheads to finish them. We always wanted to get a boat in the water as fast as we could. It was easier to move one before it was finished. When it was down in the water, level, it was easier to do the carpentry and machine work. That way, we didn't have to climb 15-18 feet up ladders and over the bulwarks to get on the boat.

At first, we were building both steel boats and wooden boats. The wooden boats were beautiful, but we couldn't sell the first one we built. We took all of our oilfield crew on it to fish the snapper banks. As soon as we got out there and anchored that round-bottomed wooden boat, it just rolled and rolled. Everybody on deck was sick, all day long. But I wasn't sick; neither were my dad and Al Silchenstedt, our naval architect and marine engineer.

At the end of the day, when we cranked up and headed home, the oil field guys began to surface. We had the fish hold full of beer and ham and cheese sandwiches. I spent my whole trip in the fish hold, handing beer up to those

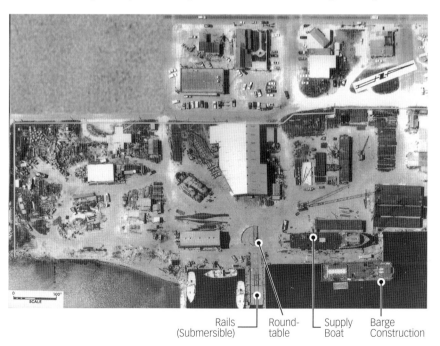

Rails (Submersible)   Round-table   Supply Boat   Barge Construction

guys. By the time we got to the dock, they were all drunk.

Not long after that, sales on our steel boats really took off. People decided that was what they needed to do. Out of 500 boats that we built in Rockport, more than 200 went to Japanese and Koreans. A lot of them went to a Japanese trading company that financed or contracted with Koreans so that basically they were Japanese/Korean boats. When we christened the boats, there'd be fifty Japanese people in town, and the boats left here with *Tokyo, Japan* painted on the fantail.

We were growing, and needed to expand. Our next door neighbor, Rob Roy Rice, had died, and in the 1960s, we bought his property in two segments. Rice's widow, Winnie, remained in their home right on the edge of their property. It was a sort of garage apartment, you might say, above a boathouse that stuck out over the water, so we left her a narrow strip of land to get to her house. Even so, that purchase greatly increased the size of our holding.

Next to Winnie's garage apartment, an old marine railway system sloped down into the water. We used it years for a time, and then the Jacksons used it for a few years—probably until the mid-60s.

We got lots of complaints from Winnie Rice. One night, she called Jim Barber, one of our foremen, and said, "You get down here! There's a shrimp boat sitting on your lift, and the engine's running. It's keeping me awake."

Jim said, "Well, lady, if it's out of the water, the engine isn't running."

"It sure is!" Winnie insisted.

So Jim drove down there in the middle of the night, and sure enough, the boat is sitting there on the lift, with the engine just idling away.

We have no idea how it started. We don't know if a cat jumped across the dash and stepped on the starter, or if something shorted something out and started it up, or what. But Winnie was right! The boat was sitting there running.

She never let us cross her yard, to get from one of our yards to the other. We had to drive a forklift or crane into the street. But the equipment didn't have license plates, so then she called the Highway Patrol, and they caught us driving on the street that way. Winnie created all kinds of problems.

Just before she died, we bought her remaining property, and we paid as much for that little strip as we had for the entire shipyard. Because she knew we had to have it.

Courtesy of Tommy Smith

When people think about RYSCO, they think about this building. It was huge—maybe 40 feet tall. We had our main office in there, with Al Silchenstedt as engineer, and Johnny Mitchell as business manager. He ran our yard in the early 1970s, when Norvell Jackson built his first steel boat. [note: N.F. Jackson, Jr., ran the shipyard warehouse in 1968.]

At the far end in the building, we had three sets of rails, so that we could frame three boats at one time. We'd lay one keel in that building, and two outside. Then we learned that we could build a boat easier outside, with winch trucks, than inside, with the overhead crane. We framed them and plated them outside, and then we took them inside, out of the wind, to weld. Then we moved them into the sandblast shed.

We built a huge dry dock for a man from Tampa. He came in with house movers, and they welded it together and launched it.

Hurricane Celia struck in 1970. Our policy, as a part of storm preparedness, was to take out into the bay any boat that was floating. We had large anchors with big flukes, to anchor them there. If a boat wasn't in the water yet, but still on the beach, we cut holes in its bottom. That way, if the water came up, the boat wouldn't float off. The water would fill it, and then run back out when the surge ebbed. We could just weld the holes back up. With steel boats, you can do things like that.

Wood boats are inexpensive and easy to maintain, but they're not very resilient, when it comes to a storm. After Celia, all the wood boats in Aransas Pass were hugging the bottom of Conn Brown Harbor. The only RYSCO boat unfit to go fishing the day after the storm was a boat that had washed up on the beach, but it wasn't damaged.

That was one of our sales pitches, and one of the reasons why people started buying steel boats. But it's hard for people to move away from what they're used to. The old shrimpers said, "I'm not gonna shrimp in a steel-housed boat; it'll be too hot. I want a wooden house." So the first steel boats that we built had wooden houses. But to build a roof that was so far up in that loft area was ridiculous and unnecessary. Steel houses were insulated and had air conditioning; they weren't

hot inside. So finally we said, "We're not building any more wood houses on our boats."

Our boats had a unique design, too. People could pick out a RYSCO boat easily; there was nothing else like it. The old Alabama fleet was square-sterned, a hex kind of a look, and a wider beam. The RYSCO boat had a wrap-around wheel house. We built a 72'x22', but not too many of them. It was expensive, and a lot more boat than a shrimper needed. One of the shrimpers had us build 68-footers, with 343 engines in them. It would pull the same nets as the 72- or 75-foot boat, but there just wasn't enough deck space to work in.

While all this was getting started, I had been in San Antonio with our oil company, but I really wasn't needed there. I was fascinated with the ship yard, so I came down here in 1973. I moved my family to a home in Corpus, and got my kids settled in school. I commuted from Corpus to Rockport every day, for about nine years, running RYSCO.

Those were really fun days, when we built all those trawlers, and it was fun going to the harbors in this area and recognizing our boats. There are a lot of shrimp boat paintings around here, too. An artist will put a name on a boat, and we can tell he wasn't really looking at the boat he was painting, because it might have a square hull, like a wooden boat, but it's got the name of one of our steel boats. You can look at the rigging, too, and it's off.

In 1975, we dredged the Rice Yard, north of my grandfather's yard, to eighteen feet in depth and bulkheaded it. We used some of the fill in the shipyard, but obviously we couldn't use it all. We pumped the rest of it over to Rockport beach. We did a huge restoration on that beach.

We pumped a ton of stuff over there, but then we kinda had an argument with the State. They wanted to charge us for the fill, but when they realized how much we were doing for the Navigation District, they came up with a price that was reasonable—just peanuts.

After a while, the rail system was in pretty bad shape. We quit using it, and after that we just used the yard as a storage area.

I bought all our engines from B. D. Holt Caterpillar, in Corpus Christi, because they were just good people. Holt was actually the inventor of the Holt Caterpillar Tractor, based in San Antonio. Holt's son Bill had a boat house here in Rockport. When Bill Holt died, his nephews Peter Holt and Holt Atherton each got a portion of the business: Holt Atherton got San Antonio, and Peter ended up with the sleepy little Corpus store. It wasn't at all setting the world on fire, but Peter was my dad's good friend. When we started building boats, we bought our engines from that Corpus store.

I met Little Peter when he came home from Viet Nam. He was wearing a Holt uniform shirt, and he'd come to our shipyard with a mechanic. Whenever we put in a new engine, they'd come over to see that it was put together right, and they'd start it up for the first time.

Holt Atherton's San Antonio store got in some trouble financially, while Peter Holt, in this little sleepy business in Corpus, was making money and not spending a lot of money. He decided to buy the Holt store in San Antonio. I read just recently that the Peter Holt Company is now the largest Caterpillar distributorship in the world. Young Peter is probably responsible for pitching it through. Big Pete was a good businessman, but I think young Pete's initiatives really moved the company along.

When I was buying Caterpillar engines, we didn't need to talk to a salesman. We just needed a line to call and say, "We need this engine, with that drive, and this power take-off, and that hydraulic drive on the back, and this type starter." That's all we needed for a marine engine.

As the demand for our shrimp boats increased, we built another shipyard in Florida. I'd buy Holt Caterpillar engines and put them on a truck for Florida, or Holt would ship them for us. We probably ordered sixty engines in one year. We furnished all the engines for the Japanese and Korean boats. Once, a guy at Caterpillar told me that RYSCO was the largest purchaser of engines in the entire United States that year.

At one time, we had 300 employees in the Rockport yard. That's when we got unionized, and we cut it down to 150. We never went over that, because when we had more employees, we had a hard time finding enough good key foremen to control the quality of our work.

When the wind blew strong, we'd catch hell about sand blasting and painting downtown Rockport and cars on the street; we'd have to pay for cleaning people's cars. There's no way anyone could do today what we did then. We painted hulls inside, but when it came to sandblasting large offshore supply boats, or painting outriggers, we had to work outside. And having to paint outside was terrible. All those epoxies were volatile, and the humidity was rough on them. We didn't want to send a boat to sea and have all the paint fall off it!

It's interesting to go around and see how other people do things that we don't do. In Paris, it's mandatory that buildings be sand-blasted every few years. They put up a scaffolding and fabric around them to contain the blasting. I wish I'd learned that when we were building boats here in Rockport.

G. "Jim" Hasslocher, who owned Jim's Restaurants, the Magic Time Machine, and other businesses in San Antonio, came down in the Eighties. He wanted to develop the Rockport Country Club that had been started by Carl Krueger and other local investors, with Larry Barnebey and Delmar Hiller selling the lots. Then he wanted us to build a gambling boat for him, building a superstructure onto a barge he had.

It was lying at the dock when a thunderstorm came through. The crew walked out the next morning, and saw the welding leads and all just hanging in the water—and no barge! They came in the office and said, "Tommy, that barge isn't there."

"What do you mean?" I asked. "What barge?"

"The *gambling* barge—Hasslocher's barge."

Courtesy of Jim Hasslocher

So I walked outside, and it's just blank. The gambling boat was the biggest thing in Rockport, five stories tall, and it was gone. We looked out across the bay and saw it, just sitting, with the sun shining through the windows.

Seventy mile per hour winds had blown that boat out into the harbor, across the bay and all the way to Mud Island (see map on page 62). It never hit anything, except for one of the entrance markers coming into Rockport that it took down. But if it had run into an oil well, it would have caused a horrible spill!

Hasslocher telephoned me when that thing blew out, but I wouldn't take his call until I talked my attorney, Bill Ellis, in Aransas Pass. "Bill," I said, "I've got some problems."

When I had explained what happened, Bill said, "Well, Tommy, wasn't that a documented barge that Hasslocher brought to the shipyard?"

"Yessir. He bought a barge in Louisiana, got it built for him to spec, documented it, and brought it in."

"Well," Bill said, "the law reads that the Barge Master is responsible for mooring the barge to the dock."

I sighed. "Oh, good!" And when Hasslocher called back, I answered the phone. He was yelling, really hacked off. "When are you going to get my barge back?"

"Well, Mr. Hasslocher," I said, "we will *assist you* in getting that barge back."

"What do you mean?"

"Well, the responsible person to have moored that barge was the Barge Master. That's *your* guy. It has nothing to do with us, whatsoever."

Boy, Hasslocher got mad. But sure enough, we assisted him; we needed the work. It wasn't helping us to have that barge sitting on Mud Island! We got hold of the tug boat people, dragged it off, and hauled it back. When Hasslocher got through tying it up, with cables and C-clamps and all that, it would have taken the whole dock with it in another blow like the one we had.

After that runaway escapade, Hasslocher decided to name his boat *Wayward Lady*. As soon as we completed our work, he took her to the Corpus Christi Marina, and docked her by Landry's. But the economy was so bad that he only kept her in Corpus for a year or two. Then he moved *Wayward Lady* to Mississippi, where it became a very profitable gambling barge.

We went into the shrimp business as tax shelters. Also, we needed to build boats at the shipyard, and when we built a spec boat, we built it for ourselves. We ended up with several different companies; my personal company owned four boats. Another company that we had, and that I was involved with, owned two. Several companies belonging to Al Silchenstedt and my dad had a couple of boats. In all, we had about ten or twelve boats, I guess—all in a distinctive, light blue color.

When we built those boats in the 1970s, we leased a property in Aransas where we put in a fuel storage tank. Edward Silchenstedt, Al's son, had some boats, so we probably had 12-14 boats fishing out of one fish house. That was quite a fleet—not huge, like Herndon in Aransas Pass, but maybe a little larger than Casterline and Jackson in Rockport-Fulton.

It wasn't long after that, that business in general "went south." With a price war, oil from Luling Oil and Gas went from $28 a barrel to $21.

We had built a couple of boats for Halliburton, and they were planning to have us rebuild their entire fleet, starting with just a couple of boats a year. We'd always have a boat in the yard, a new boat to replace an old one—from a 180-foot supply boat to a little150-foot work boat. But that changed when the price of oil dropped.

The head of Halliburton's offshore division called me from New Orleans: "I hate to tell you this. We're going to take delivery of the two boats you're building right now, but things look so bad for the future that we have enough equipment to last us for the next five years."

We were building shrimp boats too, for world fisheries. Usually, if the season was bad in the U.S., the season was great in South America or Africa. But suddenly the shrimp industry was dead. We couldn't even get repair work; that was another thing that killed us. We wouldn't haul a shrimp boat out, because we didn't need to spend a whole lot on repairs and then find out the owner couldn't pay us.

Some shipyards would haul a boat out, and let the owner work in it himself. We just couldn't fit anywhere in that category. The guys who had large boats still had some money, but we couldn't haul those boats out. It was just a disaster!

When Daddy and I flew to Florida, to the yard and back, we went right over the Gulf. Below us, we saw bayous were full of drilling rigs and supply boats—all government-guaranteed loans, Title 11 loans. So I said, "Why can't we come up with some way of putting tariffs and duties on this foreign oil, to keep the price inflated and keep our people working?"

And, as Johnny has said, shrimp boat owners and processors from Florida to Texas did organize the National Shrimp Congress, to lobby on the national and state levels.

It was amazing to see how many people were out of work across the entire Gulf coast. RYSCO laid off three hundred people—150 in each yard. It was bad, really bad. There was an "Oilman's Prayer" going around: "Oh, Lord, give us one more boom, and we promise we won't screw it up."

We started looking for a place to go to make more money. I went to Brazil and talked to a guy about moving boats to his fish company there, but decided it would be too expensive. In Florida, we started talking to people about calico scallops; we converted some of our boats and tried long-lining for swordfish.

I guess it was in the Eighties that we took the boats to Florida. Our banner year was 1984: We caught 1,700,000 gallons of calico scallops. We sold them cheaper than dog food—like $3 a gallon, for an eight-pound gallon. We had boats turning over in the harbor, loaded high with scallops. We lost one of our big boats off shore; the guys turned it over, and it went down.

Scalloping was a good deal for a while, but then turned into a disaster. When 1985 came around, the calico scallop production just fell into nothing. We never saw a year like that one. And the boats were beat up. Half of them wouldn't run.

We ended up selling the boats over there for just . . . nothing. We licked our wounds and came on home.

The next blow came when fish farming started in Central and South America. That bothered us, but not too much. Then it started in Thailand. As I understand it, fish farming is very labor intensive, and labor is very cheap in Thailand—cheaper than in South America.

One of my Japanese customers told me he was having trouble finding crews for his boats, and getting them to stay in South America, working. Older guys had been willing to go anywhere the company sent them, but the young ones didn't want to leave Tokyo. When my customer learned that his neighbors were shrimp farming, he thought, "Hey, wait a minute. Why do I want to spend $300,000 on a boat to sail to South America with six guys who don't want to go there, and won't stay there?"

He got rid of his shrimp boats, and stayed at home to farm shrimp. That happened to the industry worldwide; it just went down. And the next thing we knew, China started growing scallops. After that, there was no need for a big trawler to go out in the sea. Bubba Casterline had a boat for a long time, but I think he sold it. There are hardly any boats in Aransas Pass now; it's sickening to go over there.

We've got bundles of shrimp in the Gulf of Mexico right now, and nobody's fishing them. No one can cover the cost of that big 400 horsepower engine pulling nets, and three or four guys on board the boat. HEB Grocery Stores can sell shrimp shipped from Thailand, for less money than a Texas shrimper needs to make at the dock.

We sold our boats over a period of some years in the late Eighties. We needed to move property, just like the Jacksons did; we were in the same boat. We had some property that was basically shut down by then. The oil and gas business was down, and we were virtually out of our shipyard.

Johnny Jackson and my ex-brother-in-law, Sam Simpson, did a great job working together to get our property tied up. Then Johnny went to Perry Bass to make the deal. Since they had a close relationship, Bass was the likely one to buy the property. Sam, Jerry Wendell, and some others had already had a vision of a waterfront development plan some years earlier.

At one point, Jerry and Delo Caspary had wanted to put together a deal with us for the shipyard. They planned to go around, gradually, quietly buying up downtown Rockport—just buying individual businesses. Step by step, they could do a helluva neat development with condos, and big yachts tied up out in front, like in Florida. At the time, Wade Wendell, Jerry's son, was getting his Master's degree at the University of Texas, and he wrote his thesis on that property. Just like Johnny's plan, it was beautiful on paper, but the time wasn't ready. And it probably still isn't ready.

With the advice of an attorney, Johnny Jackson had developed a plan for us to transfer our property to them, facilitating the transfer of all the acreage to Perry Bass. After the Bass purchase, all our buildings were razed. Internationally-recognized sculptor Jesus Moroles has many items from the site in his Rockport studio: the overhead cranes, photographs, a huge table (like an over-sized chart table) with long drawers where we kept construction drawings lying flat. A lot of them were originals, drawn with a pen on Mylar. Moroles has a number of shrimp boat models, too. Most of them were built by a commercial guy in Houston, whose company name is Jimron, I think.

The Maritime Museum has two other models—a whale-backed boat, and one of our supply boats. A carpenter foreman in our shop built it, and a model of an old RYSCO trawler that I have in my home, too. I also have a model of a geophysical boat, *Cecil Green*, built by the guy in Houston.

So much of this memorabilia is a part of Rockport history. For years, we were the largest employer that Aransas County had. Maybe our old stuff can be in an Aransas County History Museum some day.

I moved to Florida and then to California. But I still have a place here; my wife Becky owns a house on a large lot on Water Street.

Johnny Jackson continues his story from this point on.

Turning the Page

The fleet was gone. The Jacksons were out of the shrimp business. I was the property manager for Perry Bass, with an office in the old bank building at Water and Main streets, adjacent to the waterfront property. I might have felt that my life was settled at last.

Whenever I had a question or needed something, I went straight to Bob Kolba, Mr. Bass' real estate guy. I had done that from the beginning of the Bass deal; I didn't need to go through his ranch foreman intermediary. But that made the ranch foreman angry, as he was a man with a huge ego. He resented me from the beginning and was always undermining me in any way he could.

I understood that the foreman was Bass' seasoned, veteran ranch guy. He had more 'stroke' than I did; he'd been around a lot longer. I was the new guy. If someone had to leave, it would be me. I didn't want to fight the foreman, because I wasn't sure that I could win.

And besides, by this time it had become very apparent to me that Mr. Bass had what I call "patient money." Eager as I was to make the waterfront development a reality, I could see that Mr. Bass had no intention to do anything with the property, any time soon. (And twenty years later, it still hasn't happened.)

So there I was, "dry docked" forever (or so I thought) at age forty-one. I was already beginning to turn gray, thanks to my first roller coaster career.

I knew that it was time for me to change careers, but I had no idea what I was going to do—not a clue.

I also realized that I had learned many valuable life lessons from my experiences in the seafood industry. I could tap the core values and life tools I had observed and developed. I took out a fresh sheet of paper and began to design a new life for myself and my family. I looked, listened, observed—seeking my new direction.

Finally, one day I happened to run into an acquaintance who was an investment advisor. "Do you mind telling me how much you make in your career?" I asked him. When my friend gave me a figure, I said to myself, "If he can do it, I *know* I can do it."

That kind of business began to intrigue me. I had never done any investing, because everything we made in the shrimp business went right back into the business. That was a bad mistake, but it's what most people do in business for themselves—reinvest in their business.

I didn't have any savings, and I didn't have any investment experience, but I did have an MBA and a lifetime of broad-based experience in the business world. I'd "been there and done that," been through the school of hard knocks. I had a good reputation and credibility in the community. I'd been involved in lots of things that I believed provided me with all the right ingredients for this new career.

I had a friend in an investment firm in Corpus Christi (let's call it Firm A), so I interviewed there first. The branch manager offered me a position for a monthly sum that would not meet more than a fraction of my bills. There was no way I could afford to work there, so I said, "Thank you, but no thank you."

I went across the street to the local office of Firm B and interviewed with the branch manager there. He seemed impressed, but said his firm required applicants to take a psychological test, predictive of success in the field. A week after I took the test, the manager called me into his office and said to me, "I'd love to hire you, but I can't."

"Why?" I asked, amazed.

"The exam says you're not going to make it in this business."

I said some expletives under my breath and left. I figuratively slammed the door and went catty-cornered across the street to the office of Pete Apple at another firm.

I had known Pete as a Presbyterian minister while I was growing up. He had since retired and gone into the investment business. He remembered me, and he had great respect for my family. So I told Pete my story.

A week later, I met with Pete's manager, John Harrell, and he hired me on the spot. He gave me three times the money I'd been offered before at Firm A. He had to pull strings to do that, but he did it, and I've never forgotten that.

So I went to work for them in February, 1992. Within three years, I was already making more money than the man who told me I'd flunked Firm B's aptitude test. That investment company has been trying to hire me ever since.

For more than two years, I commuted between my home in Rockport and my office in Corpus Christi. Then, with the support of management, I opened an office in Rockport, in the strip center shown here.

In 2008, my Rockport office moved from its first location, to our own large landscaped building, just around the corner. The photo on the next page was taken at our ribbon cutting.

My team's offices are on the first floor, and we lease suites to various concerns on the floor above.

Pat Johnson, John Jackson, Karen Mella, and Michael Farah

My Rockport office consists of a well-credentialed team with a solutions-driven business model. We offer the full-service, extensive resources and respected legacy of a worldwide firm to the comfortably retired citizens of Rockport's resort community. Retirees in Rockport and the surrounding area prefer working with a high-level advisor who is close by, and who understands their small-community way of life.

I became that qualified advisor by continuing to educate myself with skills that will help our clients. In 1999, I became the only investment advisor in all of the Coastal Bend—pretty much everything south of San Antonio and Houston—who holds the Certified Investment Management Analyst (CIMA) designation. It includes training from the Wharton School of the University of Pennsylvania and now my partner, Michael Farah, holds that designation as well.

I also hold the Accredited Investment Fiduciary (AIF) designation, qualifying me in fiduciary guidance and portfolio management. I believe I'm the only one in South Texas with that designation.

Trustees of endowments and foundations increasingly need fiduciary guidance from a qualified advisor. I have been on the boards of The Education Foundation which I originated, the Margaret Sue Rust Foundation, the Texas A&M Kingsville Foundation, the Rotary Scholarship Foundation, the Boy Scouts of America Executive Board, the Texas A&M Health Science Center Board, and the South Texas Planned Giving Council, among others. I will soon be on the Odyssey After School Enrichment Board, and I am also on the Session of the First Presbyterian Church of Rockport. All this involvement has kept me very personally aware of the challenges faced by non-profits and their trustees.

That's pretty much the story of my career, but of course my story doesn't end here. And what you've read so far is not the beginning of my family's saga, either. In the sections that follow, you'll read of historical events that led our family to this point, and I'll tell a few personal stories of the family life that made me who I am. Finally, I'll share some of the lessons I've learned, and let you in on my dream of the future for this special place that I call home. ❧

PART III
THE VOYAGE OF OUR LIFE

Land

The land that my family sold to Perry Bass was literally a piece of history. To understand that is to understand a great deal about me and my family and my hopes for the future. So I want to tell you the story of the historic slice of Texas that we once owned and occupied.

Shortly after Texas joined the United States in 1845, General Zachary Taylor sailed along Live Oak Point in Aransas Bay, looking for a good place to land. He spotted a ledge that reached all the way to the deep-water channel, forming a natural harbor, and ordered his men ashore there. From that rocky point, they marched inland about half a mile and made camp in the shade of a large live oak tree.

Some years later, John Wood recalled that Zachary Taylor had spoken enthusiastically about the rocky point. Wood believed that a wharf on the rock could be the key to successfully marketing his cattle. He and his partners built warehouses and cattle chutes on the rock and drove cattle directly from their pastures onto ships.

Before long, the Mathis cousins became agents for the Morgan Steamship line, and Morgan agreed to furnish three ships a week to handle cattle from the Rocky Point wharf.

A shipping boom would mean workers, families and businesses. Developers believed the time had come to promote a town. Naming it for the limestone ridge, they called their enterprise the town of Rockport.

In the summer of 1868, Rockport consisted of "two small wooden buildings, a cattle chute and wharf and acres of live oak bush and sage." The town "came as a mushroom in the night and at its first anniversary numbered not far from twelve hundred inhabitants." This number exceeded the entire county's population when developers first began to promote their town.

Most newcomers found temporary lodging at a hotel on the southwest corner of Water and Market streets, but no one stayed long; houses went up at an amazing rate. Soon, a string of houses ran south along Water Street. Dr. John W. Baylor built one of them—a cedar house on the beach, just far enough from the busy port.

Soon too would come Stephen Ford Jackson and Elisha H. Norvell. And our family history in Rockport would begin.

The Norvells

The Norvells originated in Scotland, and were in Virginia prior to 1630, perhaps as early as 1620. One of the pews in old Bruton Church, Williamsburg, Virginia, has a brass plate identifying Hugh and William Norvell as members of the Vestry. Hugh Norvell, a civil engineer, laid out the town of Williamsburg and was one of its incorporators.

In the "Family Album" section at the back of this book, you'll see a painting of "Riverview," the home that the Norvell family built in James City Co., Virginia, in 1683. The slave quarters in the back don't show, nor does Robert E. Lee's adjacent birthplace.

"Riverview" still faces the York River, now operating as a bed-and-breakfast and restaurant.

My great-grandfather, Elisha Hundley Norvell, was born on January 29, 1857, in Charlotte Court House, Virginia. On January 21, 1885, he married Irene Shields Barton, in Summerfield, Dallas County, Alabama. I never knew my great-grandparents, but my parents taught me to call them Nana and Dana.

Nana's grandfather, Richard Walker Barton, was born at "Shady Oaks" plantation, Frederick County, Virginia, in 1799 or 1800. He practiced law in Winchester, Virginia, where he was said to be a gifted orator. He served as a member of the U.S. House of Representatives (Whig) from 1841-43, when Daniel Webster was in the Senate.

His son, Richard Thomas Barton, was a Methodist minister who spent thirty-nine years as an educator in church schools. And he was the father of my "Nana," who was born in Lexington, Virginia, in 1865.

This photograph of Nana was taken in Selma, Alabama, in 1883-4, when she was 18 or 19 years old and teaching at Centenary Institute, a Methodist college, of which her father was President.

A year after Dana and Nana's marriage, they were both hired to teach at the Goliad Male and Female College in Goliad, Texas. Dana served as principal and teacher in the primary department; Nana taught instrumental and vocal music, painting, and drawing.

During the summer of 1888, Dana traveled from his home in Goliad to attend a political convention in Corpus Christi. He took Nana with him, and she later wrote:

> We heard so much there of Rockport, and the probability of its becoming a great port, that the gentlemen engaged passage on the Nellie Swinney, a small sailboat bound for Rockport.

I can imagine them sailing along the shoreline. They saw a well-drained sandy ridge that rested upon deep reservoirs of fresh water. It supported yaupon, mesquite, yucca and prickly pear. Wind-sculpted live oaks stood slightly inland. To the east, deep channels laced the bay, all the way to San Jose Island. Brown pelicans cruised fifty feet above the bay; gulls and terns soared, or rested on exposed reefs. Cormorants swam neck-deep. Herons and egrets strode the shallows; roseate spoonbills waded in the mud flats; shorebirds scurried. It was a beautiful place then—some might say magical. And so it remains today.

I can imagine Nana, as she looked at the new homes along the shore. "Look, Mr. Norvell!" she might have said, pointing to a small, early American cypress cottage with a modified Greek revival style front porch. "How wonderful it would be to have a home like that!"

She would later learn that Dr. John W. Baylor had built that house, and subsequently sold it to T.P. McCampbell, for $1000.00.

Left to right: Gruey, Sedan, Simon Sorenson, Norvell, and Mason

Courtesy of Aransas County Historical Society

Nana was a prolific writer, so I will entrust much of this story to her capable hand:

There was only one small hotel in Rockport, known as the Congdon House, on the beach. Mr. and Mrs. Dick Wood boarded there, and but for her companionship I suspect I would have had a dreary time, because the house was crowded with men, all excited over "Deep Water," real estate, &c., and my husband caught the fever. His grandfather, Elisha Estes Hundley, had made a fortune in real estate in Chicago, so he had always wanted to try it, and decided this would be a good opportunity to get in on the ground floor.

Mr. Norvell spent the summer in Rockport and I visited him one week. It was there that I met Mr. and Mrs. George Fulton when they came in from their Rincon Ranch.

We were planning to move to Rockport in the fall, and Papa, not wanting to be separated from us, decided to follow us. When we moved the latter part of August, 1888, we could then reach Rockport on the train. Mr. Norvell had rented the T. P. McCampbell home on the Beach, and a year later bought it for $2000.00.

Nana's father (my great-great grandfather), moved in with them. As soon as everyone was settled, Nana went to San Antonio and bought a piano. She put an ad in the *Aransas Pass Beacon* soliciting music pupils for herself and boys for her father's classical school, and they soon had applications.

Professor Barton hardly had his school opened when the public school began. Its trustees asked him to be Superintendent, and he was ready to accept—until the Trustees told the professor he could not read scripture or pray in the school. In the end, a compromise allowed Professor Barton to repeat the Lord's Prayer and read the Bible so long as he made no comment on it.

Nana's students gave recitals for invited guests—in her home for the first three years. Then, after the Bailey Pavilion was built, she had the recitals there.

On the 14th of March, 1891, Irene [my grandmother, named for her mother] *was born. Then the music lessons were laid aside for a while, and the busy life of being a Mother began, and the interesting study of watching the development of a child, mentally and physically.*

Mr. Norvell was Extension Agent for the SA&AP (San Antonio and Aransas Pass) Railroad, and for several years he took exhibits from this section and displayed them at the Fair in San Antonio. As we could get passes on the R.R., we looked forward each year to that little outing.

As my Grandmother grew, she began to form her own memories of Rockport in this period. A 1963 interview with her in the *Corpus Christi Caller-Times*, quotes her:

Rockport was a boom town in the 1890s, with one main street and no paving. Horse drawn buggies were used as transportation. Rockport also had one mule-drawn streetcar. It ran all the way to Oklahoma—a small development seven miles south of Rockport.

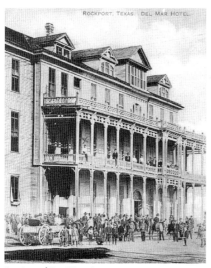

Courtesy of Kam Wagert, from her postcard collection

Grandmother said that her father was the "ram rod" for the railroad's weekend excursions to Rockport. *People flocked to Rockport to spend the weekend. The train fare to Rockport from San Antonio was $2.50. At that time we had two large hotels. One was the Aransas, which had four stories and could accommodate 100 couples on the dance floor.* (Note: This building was also known as the Del Mar Hotel. Its fourth floor 'rooms' were decorative effects, and not used for guests.)

But two hotels were not enough. The crowds were so large, people stayed in homes or any spare bed or couch they could find. Beds were 50 cents for the weekend.

The people fished, swam and danced on the big bathing pavilions that were built out over the water.

ROCKPORT, TEXAS,
IN THE GOOD OLD SUMMER TIME.

Courtesy of Kam Wagert,
from her postcard collection

SHIP YARD AND FISH FLEET
AT ROCKPORT, TEXAS.

Boat on chocks   Haul-out ways

Courtesy of Kam Wagert, from her postcard collection

Elisha decided to get into the real estate business. His wife now picks up the story of their family life:

> As Irene advanced in years, I began to teach her the regular school course, and also was regular with her music lessons. I started out with the rule that she was never to refuse when asked to play, and she never did. One evening, for an encore, she sang and played an old ballad that she had taken a fancy to and learned herself.

Nana was among the ladies of Aransas who joined Twentieth Century Club, organized by the wife of Judge Baldwin. Nana wrote: "We confined our studies almost entirely to Shakespeare, only one year each to Mythology and Texas History." The club flourished for many years. Nana is credited with introducing the game of Charades to the crowd at the Bailey Pavilion, and she wrote for various newspapers over the years.

A neighbor, Winifred Lowther, was a writer too, and published a contemporary history, *The Old Beach Road*. In it, she wrote of Nana: "Mrs. Norvell ... whose

ROCKPORT, TEXAS. PAVILION.

family traditions went deep into the English aristocracy, brought her inherited code of living . . . to this small remotely-situated town."

It might have sounded like a compliment, but she went on to state that Mrs. Norvell was not inclined to visit or meet socially with people of another class.

It seems to be true that Nana didn't know much about her next-door neighbors, the Hanks family. She knew only that Mr. Hanks was a saloon keeper, and for that reason Nana stayed somewhat aloof—but she knew when to break the code.

Mrs. Hanks' sister, who lived with the family, died of consumption, and Nana went next door to offer help and sympathy. She was rebuffed.

"For years now," Mrs. Hanks said, "we have managed without knowing our next door neighbor; there is no need of knowing her now."

Nana had to acknowledge that her inbred exclusiveness required alteration. After that, Winifred Lowther's book included her opinion that the "change in this Virginia family made them more admirable and likable than before."

Nana's daughter Irene (my grandmother) was a member of the first graduating class of Rockport High School, the class of 1907. She later told a reporter, "There were six in my graduating class—two boys and four girls. Since there was no auditorium at the school, we had our graduating ceremonies at the Bailey bathing pavilion."

Irene proceeded to the San Antonio Female College, now Trinity University. "How we hated the word *female* in the school's name. The school faculty was very strict. When we went anywhere, we marched in a group and were chaperoned.

When we were out in a group, we couldn't speak to anyone we knew without permission from our chaperones."

Dating was unheard of: "We couldn't even cut our eyes at a boy. There were three boys' schools in San Antonio then, and three or four times a year, our school had a reception and invited the boys.

"Sometimes, the boys gave us the insignia patches off their uniforms. We had more fun wearing them around the school. Of course we were not supposed to, and if we were caught, the patches were taken away from us."

Grandmother majored in English and minored in history at the two year school. Then, as a graduate student, she returned to study piano for two more years.

When Dana and Nana learned that their daughter Irene planned to marry S. F. Jackson, they had a house built at 801 North Magnolia Street. In 1914, they gave it, as a wedding present, to the young couple (who would later be my grandparents). Daddy was born in that house the next year, and it would be the house that my sister, brothers, and I were raised in. Daddy and Mother lived there until 1973.

The Jacksons

We can trace our Jackson family tree back to William de Bolling, an English landowner in 1165. In the Americas, our lineage includes John Rolfe and Pocahontas.

My great-grandfather, James Andrew Jackson, was born in Coosa County, Alabama, and became a member of the first graduating class at the Texas Agriculture and Mechanical College (now Texas A&M University). My brother Bobby reports that this Jackson "practically built the town of Pasadena, Texas"; there are schools and streets named for him.

Roy Jackson, my great uncle, came to Rockport to look at the seafood business. There was no real harbor then, but he saw that the rocky point provided plenty of protection.

Small-scale fishing and oystering had been a part of the Rockport scene since the mid-1800s. In 1888, David Rockport Scrivner began operating Miller Brothers' Fish Company in Fulton. His fleet of three or four fishing scows—sailboats—easily brought in two or three thousand pounds of fish at a time.

Scrivner had to spend a lot time on the road, trying to establish markets for his fish, and he must have been a good salesman. Soon, he opened a second fish house in Rockport, and when he'd been in business nineteen years, he had one hundred and seventy men working on his thirty-two boats—sail-driven trawlers that worked only in the bays, not in the Gulf.

Roy Jackson decided to buy Scrivner's thriving seafood business, and he renamed it Jackson Fish Company. His brother, my grandfather Stephen Ford Jackson, joined the business a few years later and became an executive. In 1905, the company name changed its name to Jackson Brothers Company.

Jackson Brothers sent oysters North by train in iced wooden barrels, and the oysters were featured on menus in San Antonio, Dallas, and Chicago. The barrels stayed around our fish house for many years; my brother N.F. remembers playing in them.

At the end of each week, the Jackson brothers cleared the floor of their fish house and held dances for the community. Local fiddlers provided the music and the ladies brought coffee and cake. Young couples put their children to bed atop the ice boxes.

My grandfather, S.F. Jackson, bought the business from his brother in 1919. Roy had lost a son to drowning, and never got over it, so he wanted to move to Sinton. There he established one of the first automobile dealerships in South Texas and also became a banker. (In an old newspaper, I saw an ad for Jackson Brothers Ford dealership too, but I have no information about it at all.)

At about that same time, Jim Tuttle threw out a hand net in Aransas Bay and hauled in shrimp. Some men were already catching shrimp near Corpus Christi, but no one realized the wealth of them around Rockport and Fulton. Soon shrimpers worked two sailboats side by side, dragging large nets between them. My Grandfather Jackson got into that business too.

My Grandparents

We called our grandfather, Stephen Ford Jackson, "YaYa." One of his first grandchildren called him that, and soon everyone else followed suit. Almost everyone, that is. Our grandmother called him "Ford," and her mother, Irene Barton Norvell, referred to him as "Ford" in her memoir. For business purposes, of course, YaYa was known as S.F.

My uncle Bruce Davis, the family's tireless genealogist, knew YaYa well, and described him this way: "He stood about 6'1" tall, with dark brown hair and brown eyes. He was habitually a calm and quiet man who commanded attention and respect but did not invite undue familiarity. In his later years, with firm monetary security, he continued to live plainly and without ostentation."

YaYa married Irene Norvell on June 25, 1913. We called her "Grandmother," making her the only elder member of the family who didn't have a nickname.

But she was such a quintessential lady that "Grandmother" suited her best.

YaYa and Grandmother had five children—my father Norvell Ford (right, in top right photo below), then James Barton, Isabel Irene, Annie Ruth, and Mary Virginia.

With such a large family, YaYa and Grandmother moved from their little wedding house, just one block south, to a white, two-story home still standing at 701 North Magnolia Street.

That house had been built in 1900 by a member of the Wood family—a descendant of the man who first began development on the rocky point. For years, Grandmother had a beautiful yard—the garden spot of Rockport.

THE HERALD FOOTBALL PREVIEW – PAGE 43

Rockport's First Football Team, 1931 (Top Row L-R) E. M. Dunn, Coach and Principal, Cecil (Spec) Smith, Bernard Fox, Jerry Picton, Lyle Diederich, Edward Barnard, Jesse Owens, Pat Mixon, Manager, organizer, and Assistant Coach; (Front Row L-R) Billy Mowers, Jim Jackson, Mike Townsend, Norvell Jackson, Bill Gray (Photo Courtesy of Pat and Joel Mixon)

The back of the house faced Rockport School. When my dad and his brother were attending it, and playing football, the attic of their house became the team's field house; all the uniforms hung there.

Grandmother organized the Rockport and Fulton Parent-Teacher Associations and served as President of the Rockport PTA five different times. "I always took the job when no one else wanted it," she said. Grandmother was instrumental in organizing the Rockport High School Alumnae Association, served on the executive board of the Aransas County Red Cross during World War II, was chairman of the Aransas County Cancer Crusade, a Matron of the Order of the Eastern Star, a member of the Aransas County Woman's
Club, on the executive board of the Women of the First Presbyterian Church and the Rockport Cemetery Association Board, and an auxiliary member of the board of the Aransas County Public Library. She was a member of the Daughters of the American Revolution until she resigned in protest for that organization's refusal to let Marian Anderson sing in the Washington, D.C. auditorium.

In the 1950s-60s, Grandmother was the Aransas County correspondent and historical writer for the *Corpus Christi Caller-Times* and a member of the Corpus Christi By-Liners' Club. She told a latter-day *Caller-Times* reporter: "I wrote everything from weddings to wrecks. I went to many fires and one tavern brawl, but I stayed outside the tavern."

My grandfather, S.F. Jackson, served as president of the school board for twenty years. He served two terms as Mayor of Rockport. The situation leading up to his election, as detailed in the Minutes of the City Council, is interesting reading, digested here, with direct quotes in italics.

On April 19, 1921, the current Mayor, A.R.A. Brice, was absent. *The secretary was instructed to write to Mayor Brice, asking for a detailed statement of what was known as The Mayor's Special Fund and originally amounting to $1748.70, same to be here not later than May 1st.*

On May 17, William Mayer, Mayor Pro-tem *authorized to transfer the Account at the First National Bank, known as the "Mayor's Extra Special Fund" to the credit of the City's Street Fund.... The letter of Mayor Brice, tendering his resignation, under date of April 27th, was read and accepted.*

On March 7, 1922, *Election notices for a Mayor* and two Aldermen *were posted at Court house, Post Office and Bank and notice for publication left with editor,* Pilot.

Minutes on April 4: *The Mayor Pro-tem appointed Gibson and Prophet to canvass the votes of the City Election held this day. The committee after canvassing the votes reported the following results, found according to the returns of the election*:

S.F. Jackson received 158 votes for Mayor

WW Winslow received 42 votes for Mayor

. . . Accordingly the Mayor Pre-tem declared that S. F. Jackson . . . receiving the majority of the votes [was] *duly elected.* He was sworn in on April 18, 1922. *It was unanimously resolved by the newly elected Mayor and the Board to give, for the good of the City, their services without compensation: placing the salary of each at one dollar per year.*

My grandfather's first order of business as Mayor was to pass an ordinance authorizing the issuance of Breakwater bonds of and by the City in the sum of $50,000.

On April Fool's Day, April 1, 1924, S.F. was re-elected for a second term. He ran unopposed and garnered 84 votes. From the results in other races on that day, it appears that only 84 voters cast ballots—a significant drop from the 200 votes cast two years earlier.

Near the end of his second term, on March 2, 1926, Mayor S. F. Jackson, *by authority of the Board called an election to be held first Tuesday in April, the sixth, for the election of a Mayor. Secretary instructed to have notice of said election published in the* Pilot *four times. Mr. E. H. Norvell* (S.F.'s father-in-law) *was appointed presiding judge.*

On April 4, J. Ed. Moore and Amos Glass tied for the position of Mayor. S. F. Jackson declared the election void, and called a Special election to decide the issue within ten days. At a called meeting April 14, Moore edged out Glass, 104 to 92, *and the Mayor declared Mr. Moore elected mayor for the ensuing term of two years.*

My grandfather also served as president of the Chamber of Commerce, Worshipful Master of Masonic Lodge

#323, an elder in the Presbyterian Church, and president of the Texas Fisheries Association.

After World War II, my grandfather's two sons—Norvell Ford Jackson (my father, on the right, previous page) and James Barton Jackson (my Uncle Jim, next to his father)—became a part of Jackson Seafood. They spent long, grueling hours in that fish house by the bay; the business was their life for many, many years.

My Father

Norvell Ford Jackson was born in Rockport on June 29, 1915, in the house at 801 North Magnolia, where his own children would later grow up. Daddy lived in Rockport all his life. He was the first second-generation graduate of Rockport High School in 1932, and a member of the first high school football team in Rockport. My dad was one hell of an athlete—six foot tall and weighing two hundred pounds. I heard that, in 1932, he ran the hundred yard dash, on grass, in 9.9 seconds.

Since Rockport schools were not yet accredited, Daddy started college at Schreiner Institute, in Kerrville, where he played full back on their football team. At that time, football players didn't have the protective gear they do now. Their helmets didn't have a face guard or anything; basically a player just had leather on top of his head. One day, someone tried to tackle Daddy and he lowered his head, knocking the tackler out. From then on, Daddy was known as "Iron Head."

After receiving an Associate in Arts degree from Schreiner in 1934, Daddy went on to Rice University, where he ran track. He then attended The University of Texas, where he completed his collegiate career. Of course his "Iron Head" nickname followed him to UT.

Daddy was a member of the Phi Theta Kappa Fraternity, and the Delta Theta Phi Law Fraternity (even though he wasn't studying law). He met John Connally there and also became friends with Harvey Weil, (who would later be our attorney in the property dispute with the Navigation District).

Daddy graduated with a Bachelor of Business Administration in Marketing in 1938. After college, he returned to Rockport—but he chose not to go into the family seafood business yet. He had a business of his own—Jackson Sales Company—right down town, on Austin Street.

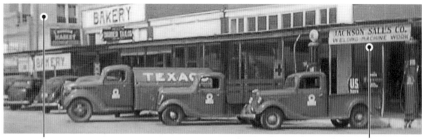

Sorenson Bldg.
(Estelle Stair gallery)

Jackson
Sales Company

Daddy was a consignee of the Texaco Oil Company; they provided him fuel, and he didn't have to pay for it until he sold it. He had pumps there on Austin Street, but it wasn't a gas station, selling to individuals; he sold only to the trade. He also had a fuel truck in which he made deliveries to businesses and boats.

In 1939, the *Rockport Pilot* front page had a large headline that read:

Norvell F. Jackson is Outstanding as Young Rockport Business Man
Heads Jackson Sales Company, One of City's Leading Firms

The story informed readers that "N.F. Jackson is . . . only twenty-four years of age, but well qualified to identify himself among the business leaders of the city." The *Pilot* added that Daddy was "successfully operating a firm which is so varied in its lines as well as vast in its size that ordinarily one would imagine it to be guided by an old and experienced head."

He held the wholesale consignee rights of all Texaco products covering Aransas County and San Patricio County up to Gregory; was a key dealer for Firestone Tire and Rubber Company; was authorized for Ford repair, parts and service, with a complete general garage manned by trained mechanics; and ran a welding and machine shop business.

That same year, Nazi Germany invaded Poland; France and Great Britain declared war on Germany. But for most people in Rockport, the conflict seemed very far away. Daddy was seeing Neva Miles Porter, of Gonzales, Texas, and they married on October 30, 1940.

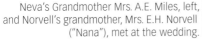
Neva's Grandmother Mrs. A.E. Miles, left, and Norvell's grandmother, Mrs. E.H. Norvell ("Nana"), met at the wedding.

Then, on December 7, 1941, Japan bombed Pearl Harbor. Within a week, the U.S. found itself fighting wars in Europe and the Pacific.

Rockport, recognizing its vulnerability as a coastal town, planned practice blackouts. Floyd Huffman (who had drawn the plat of our property a year or two earlier) and my dad served as observers atop the courthouse.

As the government encouraged civilians to eat more seafood, and meat rationing cut homemakers' choices, the shrimping business boomed. Texas harvested eighteen million pounds of shrimp in 1942, up by a third in only six years.

On Thursday, January 28, 1942, the *Rockport Pilot* published an Extra edition, warning that a German submarine had been sighted in the Gulf of Mexico. The practice blackout set for that evening suddenly changed to an all-night wartime precautionary measure.

By summer, Daddy had enlisted in the Army Air Force. Mr. Hugh Morrison, who was older, did not enlist, so Daddy asked him to run his Texaco business, while he was in the service.

But no one could take his place at home; his wife was expecting their first child. Daddy's goodbyes held a new element of sadness as he headed to Sheppard Field, in Pueblo, Colorado.

Daddy wrote more than ninety letters to his mother during the war, and she saved them all. The first letter was dated July 13, 1942, from Sheppard Field, and the last September 11, 1945, just before Daddy's formal discharge from a base in Alamogordo, New Mexico.

All the letters begin "Dear Folks," followed by an apology for how long it had been since he wrote last. (But the letters usually were only a week or two apart.) Daddy was rather articulate, and I am amused by some of his expressions and humor at times. Some of the things I remember him saying in later life showed up even in these letters written when he was young.

He always filled a whole page. Never one to waste anything, not even paper, he would write "Love, Norvell, on the last quarter inch of paper,

He mentions "Momma" more frequently than "Daddy." He was constantly aware of how much Grandmother and YaYa were helping his family and business.

He often mentions writing to my mother Neva, and how he missed her: *There is practically no possibility that I can be there when the baby is born. Don't want to tell Neva now . . . in all probability I'll be in California at the time.*

Then: *Thanks for all you've done for Neva and me. . . I was ready to start yelling. . . All I know is that we had a daughter named Mary Lucille, born October 30, 1942. Still wondering how big she was and what she looked like . . . I can't do much 'bragging' without some more details. . . Up to now all I have to go on is that she's a "precious little monkey."*

He saw her once, when she was six weeks old, and he was riding a transport train across country. Mary Lucille heard the story so many times that she believed she actually remembered being with him.

The War Board censored portions of Daddy's overseas letters, but by piecing bits of information together, we've come to the conclusion that his 506th 44th Squadron, Bomber Group was based at Shipdham Field, in England.

He wrote of how much he missed his little Mary Lucille, adding: *"If Neva or the baby need anything, see to it they have it and I'll pay you back somehow, sometime.* Daddy was very conscious of sending money home and taking care of his family.

In all his letters, Daddy's personality came through loud and clear: his Christian upbringing, his family values and ethics, his work ethic. He never whined and seldom complained about anything, but it was easy to see that he felt homesick.

He attended an Episcopal Church when he could. He shopped for gifts to send home. While on leave in London, he attended dozens of "shows"—Irving Berlin's "This is the Army," Fred Astaire in "The Sky's the Limit."

He referred to Neva's continuous story of Mary Lucille's sore throat, cold, and finally measles. *I'm afraid she will be past all this when I see her again. It's hard* to imagine her—*I still remember as she was at 6-10 weeks.* And later he states that his prized possession is a lock of his daughter's hair.

He obviously was not a partier and seldom left the base. The trips that he did make were primarily to London, sometimes Ireland, and occasionally Belgium. He particularly enjoyed a trip to Scotland.

Daddy really liked his base. He seemed to be comfortable, well fed, and healthy. *I ate nine eggs at once about two months ago—milk and ice cream—almost forgot fried chicken.* He bragged about the Red Cross; they seemed to be everywhere.

Daddy really took to his classes and training in aircraft mechanics; he seemed to really enjoy and excel at it. *Can't talk about my work. . . Went to a school and finished with a grade of 95, top of the class.*

He seemed to view the war as "work" rather than "battle"—probably since he never flew on missions and wasn't really in harm's way. Enjoying new work, he wrote: *"Was told I was doing more than my share on part of it and will discontinue hitting it quite that hard. . . . Still hope to get an assistant.* Daddy was always someone who did more than his share; that's the way he was in everything he did all his life.

To his father he wrote: *So happy to know that you have an oil well.* The well was on property my grandfather owned in Taft, and the family got small royalties from it for years.

Daddy's letter to his father continued: *It's high time you both took a rest from your job of bringing up a family. Maybe after the war is over, we can shift for ourselves. But without you both, I don't know how my family or business could ever have gotten along so well.*

Later: *When I received your last letter, I never thought I'd be answering it from Africa. I'm roughly twice as far from the States as I've ever been. At Tunis, I ate the first ice cream I've had since the States. It's hot; we try to dress as cool as possible, but the natives cover up.*

He cabled Neva when he could tell her he was back "home" safely. *Glad to be back in London. I slept in the first bed in a month.*

Learning from Neva that his grandmother, Irene Norvell, whom we later called Nana, had died, Daddy wrote: *I can't seem to find words to express my feelings . . . about the most loving grandmother a fellow ever had.* He borrowed

Shipdham Field

Norvell on right, as Aircraft Inspector, Shipdham Field, England ("Fearless Fosdick" was a character in Al Capp's "Li'l Abner" newspaper comic strip.

instead words that Neva had written about Irene: *With her passing God has taken to himself one of the most saintliest creatures he ever put on this earth . . . and one of the most talented and most beloved. Not a one of us would have kept her back, though, for her work was ended and her strength gone. In the few short years that I've known her, she has become my grandmother, too, and the great grandmother of our precious daughter, and I have loved her more than anyone knows.*

In the spring of 1944, Daddy wrote of 25 attacks in 31 days, and: *RAF last night, giving Hitler a headache!*

He mentions that he had been offered "two pounds" for his alarm clock: *May sell if it goes much higher.* Two months later: *I'm pretty mighty tired of this stay over here. . . Most of all, tired of my job and being away from home. . . I hope that a complete history is printed when this is over, so that the entire truth will come out and take some of the glory from the Fortresses* [B-17s] *and lend it to the Liberators* [B-24s].

In July: *Still monotonous. Listening to news that B29s have bombed Japan. I want to finish my trip around the world when Germany is through and hope to see some B24's bomb Japan also.*

In October, 1944, he heard of his father's illness: *Never occurred to me to be worried that anything was wrong until I learned that Daddy had quite a serious time. I understand he's out of danger now, and I pray that's true. Hope this finds him in good health again and that he has come to the conclusion to take life a little easier. I told Neva I was going to insist he sell the business and not to have any thought or worry about us. Please listen to us and take it easy.*

In December: *I haven't too much to gripe about—just don't like the Army, don't like England, and don't like to be away from home. I keep thinking it won't be many more months.*

January, 1945: *Because we knew we could be so much more comfortable than in the barracks, a couple of crew chiefs and I decided to build a house on the line near work. We weren't satisfied with the one-room shacks that others had, so built a two-room job with bath. It took a little less than a month to build, made of about 200 munitions boxes. It's comfortable—better than a lot of homes over here. We made a stove, have electric lights, all the necessary furniture—even a radio speaker that is connected to the radio in a neighbor's shack.*

April: *I'm just about convinced that the Air Corps won't return to the States for a long time and I'm not very anxious to be in an occupation Air Force.*

Our community [of shacks] *has progressed. We now have a horseshoe pit in the "square" and a volleyball court in the park. Have fun each night listening to the "Villagers" repeat the rumors they have picked up during the day. I guess there is no place like the Army to get rumors unless it's the States, which has just prematurely celebrated the Germans' surrender.*

May 7, 1945: *I'm not particularly anxious to take a pass now that the celebration is scheduled to start tomorrow. It seems so useless to celebrate as far as we are concerned. The war has been over for us for a long time now.*

Finally, Daddy was stateside once more. In July, he wrote from Alamogordo NM: *How hopeless this base is. I'm doing absolutely nothing but eating up the government's food. Thousands of us doing the same thing here and throughout the 34 bases in the 2nd Air Force. The Army confusion and inefficiency I've seen is multiplied 100 times here.*

I wish I could be back working on the gas business now that rationing is over. Daddy, wouldn't it be advisable to let the public know of your plans for a freezing plant before someone else has similar plans!

September 24, 1945: *I expect my discharge about a week from today.*

The thing that impressed me most is reading a day-by-day accounting of part of Daddy's young adulthood, written through his eyes, when he was less than half as old as I am today.

He was mature and had his head on straight. He was strongly connected to his family and lived a life of strong, decent moral values and plain old hard work. He passed that extreme work ethic on to me, my brothers N.F. and Bobby, and my sister, Mary Lucille. It has often been said that this was the greatest generation, and I'm convinced that is indeed true.

When Daddy and Uncle Jim returned from the war, they started buying war surplus hulls and diesels to start a new fleet of boats. Our *Charlotte* and *Luka* were Army surplus hulls, and I think the Quonset hut on our property was actually a war surplus kit.

Then, when I was about ten years old, my grandfather, my dad, and Uncle Jim leased the adjacent Rice shipyard land under a corporation called Jackson Marine Services, Inc. While my uncle continued to run the shrimp company, my dad ran that shipyard, where we had a haul-out boat repair facility, and also did sandblasting and painting.

My mom and dad both worked there, and I did too, during summers while I was in junior and senior high school. My dad ran the rail 'ways'—a haul-out for big shrimp boats and ferry boats and barges up to 60 or 70 feet in length, and some maybe longer.

For a while, we built boats too.

All of that turned out to be a tough business, and I suspect it was marginal at best, since they decided to exit the shipyard business after only a few years.

Daddy, Mary Lucille, Mother

Daddy was a man of great physical stature—all muscle, with the toughest and strongest hands. He was always working with his hands, and I think that's how he stayed in such good physical shape. Mother called him her Adonis.

The most common vision I have of Daddy is in clothes soaking wet with sweat, and dirty hands. He usually came home for a short nap at noon, but still in those sweaty, dirty clothes.

Although Daddy was an educated man, I would characterize him more as a "doer" than as a "deep thinker." He was short on talk, long on walk, and was not particularly comfortable behind a desk.

That's not to say he wouldn't express his opinion. He often was forceful about things he believed in strongly. He could sometimes be a somewhat tough boss with employees, and he stood his ground with those who disagreed with him. I often marveled at how even those people still expressed the utmost respect for him. They knew that, when times got tough, he could be counted on.

Bobby and N.F. both remember, as I do, that Daddy got up and went to work at 4:30 in the morning, and often didn't get home until after we went to bed. Sometimes, when it wasn't busy, Daddy would come home and eat dinner. But if there was a boat in, or something, he'd stay at work. Mother would sometimes take us kids and a picnic basket to the fish house, and we'd eat at Daddy's desk. He would come in from unloading boats to grab a bite with us. Daddy worked from before sun up until late every night, and these dinners on the desk were the only time we got to see him at times.

Bobby adds, "I always knew I would see him on Sunday, because he never missed church. That's what he and Mother taught me, too. When I was in high school, my parents would say, 'You can go and stay out all night. If you do drink, just be careful. But you be there, in the pew, at eleven o'clock on Sunday morning'."

Daddy led by doing. His real motivation to others was that he rolled up his sleeves and did something about a problem. In times of emergency and crisis, he just reacted quickly, seemingly without thinking sometimes, and did what was needed.

I guess some people feared him. He could be gruff, and he was very demanding with his employees. He was the hardest working man I've ever known. He could do the work of ten men.

Daddy would never ask an employee to do something he would not do himself—and in fact he often did. Once, a shipyard worker was putting the chafing on the bottom of one of our wood hulls that had been hauled out, and Daddy walked up. With obvious disapproval, he said, "Get out of the way son; I'll just do that myself."

The worker replied, "But Mr. Jackson, you might as well let me do it because you're paying me for it anyway."

Daddy shook his head. "I don't care. Go ahead and bill me."

Another time, Daddy was at the bottom of a bilge, cleaning it, while two guys he was paying stood there and watched. That kind of thing went on all the time.

Joe Barrera told me about a winter day when they had to haul a boat out. The boat and cradle were down in water so cold that steam was rising off it. Then the sheave broke, or the haul-out cable got twisted or something, and they couldn't winch the boat out. While everybody else stood around looking, Daddy stripped off his shirt and watch and shoes and started walking out into the ice cold water. When he got to the cradle, he went underwater for what seemed like five minutes or so.

When Daddy finally came up, swam to shallower water, and started walking out, the steam was rolling off his body. The workers just stood there, jaws dropped in disbelief.

Daddy looked at them and said, "What are you standing there for? Let's haul this boat out!" After that, the employees called him the man of steel.

Once, he was at the wheel of one of our boats, the *Little Tony*, towing another boat, when the tow rope got caught in the wheel. The *Little Tony* heeled way over. It not only capsized, but did a complete three-sixty underwater and then righted itself. The whole time, Daddy stayed at the wheel. And later, he never talked about it; I heard the story from others who saw it. I guess Daddy wanted to keep the story from my mother.

My father was a very generous man. Often, he didn't have a lot to give monetarily, but he was extremely unselfish with his time, and especially with his physical effort. No matter how tired or broke he might be, if any family member so much as hinted at needing help, Daddy would be there without being asked.

Bobby said, "I knew he was there for me no matter what. The only time he would drop what he was doing in the business, was when someone in his family needed him. There wasn't anything—anything—he wouldn't do for his kids, throughout his entire life."

Daddy always wanted to be productive, never idle. And now, I realize I'm exactly like him. Except for the fifteen minute nap he religiously took every day after lunch, Daddy was always doing something. He spent thousands of hours on work days at the church, at Scout camp, or simply on busy work at the deer lease.

The First Presbyterian Church of Rockport was a central focus of my father's life. His grandparents were charter members of the church, and the Norvell ancestors had been Presbyterians back in Scotland. Daddy was baptized at Rockport's First Presbyterian, and raised there. In adulthood, he served the Lord and his church faithfully as a deacon and ruling elder. He was a member of the board of Mo Ranch, a Presbyterian retreat in the Hill Country. He somehow found time to serve on Presbytery and Synod boards and committees.

The Boy Scouts of America was another of my dad's great passions. He couldn't be an active troop leader because of the seven-days-a-week demands of the business, but he served on the committee of Troop 49 of Rockport for many years, and on the Executive Board of the Gulf Coast Council. He was conferred the James E. West Fellowship honor for his lifelong contributions to Scouting. He received the prized Silver Beaver Award and was a Vigil Honor Member of the Order of the Arrow.

Daddy gave much back to Rockport. He was a member of the local Rotary Club, a member and Assistant Chief of the Rockport Volunteer Fire Department, a member of the Rockport VFW Post #3902, a commissioner and chair of the Aransas County Navigation District, and for many years an alderman and Mayor Pro-Tem on the Rockport City Council. He also served on numerous city and county commissions and was a director of the Live Oak State Bank.

But Daddy's greatest source of pride was his family; his greatest joy came from witnessing the achievements and accomplishments of his children and grandchildren. He loved the occasions when all his family was around. No sacrifice was ever too great for his family.

Daddy was raised with a deep and traditional sense of values, and by quiet example, he instilled his bedrock values in all of us.

I guess the times I felt closest to him were when we went hunting together, sitting quietly in a deer blind with no one else around. He showed me how to shoot a rifle and field dress a deer. In this photo, I'm showing off my first buck, when I was about twelve years old.

Daddy educated me a lot about life, beyond the example of values he set. He taught me basic, every day things—how to handle a winch truck, and how to move a 100-ton boat around the docks. He showed me the difference between a cap screw and a carriage bolt or machine bolt, or a street ell, a bushing or a reducer.

When I try to describe my dad, the first word that always comes to mind is "rock." Daddy was unfettered, fearless, determined, unmovable in his faith and conviction, enduring.

My Mother

Mother's father (John Duncan Porter, but "Poppy" to us) was a school teacher. He taught "industrial arts," a variety of vocational things. He played minor league baseball, too. But after being injured during a game, he was unable to work for a while during the Depression. Although the family moved around some, Mother and her siblings considered Gonzales, Texas, their home. After Poppy retired from teaching, he worked as a house painter.

Our Grandmother Porter, whom we called "Mom," was the daughter of a degreed engineer, who built dams and bridges. "Mom" was born in a sod house in Indian Territory, near what is now Ada, Oklahoma. The family lived in tents at construction sites.

My mother, Neva Miles Porter was born on November 18, 1919, in Mineral

Wells, Texas. From her varied background, it may not be so surprising that she turned out to be a multi-talented woman. She sang in variety shows and played the piano and organ. She received a full scholarship to the University of California at Redlands, studying music, majoring in performing arts and vocal arts.

She had a boyfriend out there, John Raitt. They sang together, on stage at the Hollywood Bowl. But when Raitt proposed to Mother she turned him down.

He became a famous Broadway star and the father of singer Bonnie Raitt. Mother came back to Texas, where a friend, Verna Haseman, introduced her to Norvell Jackson, and they married in 1940.

While Daddy was gone to the war, Mother and Mary Lucille moved to Austin to be near her family. Mary Lucille, the oldest granddaughter on both sides of the family—the Porters and the Jacksons—was practically raised by her uncles. How she was doted on by the relatives! She was the queen bee.

Mother continued her studies in Performing Arts at UT, determined to make all A's. She got in with a local radio station, where she did commercial jingles, and sometimes she would sing.

And she (2nd from left in photo above right) had a radio show with Cactus Pryor, who would later become a legend in Texas broadcasting and entertainment. As I understand it, he was just a student then, as she was; I don't think he had made a name for himself yet. They did stories—like little plays.

Daddy was still overseas when Mother graduated from college, Phi Beta Kappa. She was credited with naming the "Surf" movie theater in Rockport, and she had a hand in designing the fish logo for the Chamber promoting our area as "The Toast of the Coast."

Throughout her life, so busy with her family, Mother still found time to express her artistic side. When world renowned artist Simon Michael came to town, his first studio was in the house behind our home at 801 N. Magnolia, and Mother was one of his first pupils. Michael founded an art school in Fulton in 1948, but just two years later, he purchased five acres on King Street, in Rockport, and moved his school there. In 1959, Mother was chosen artist of the month by the Corpus Christi Fine Arts Colony. N.F. remembers helping her hang her show—all pastels—and they remained on display throughout the month of January.

One time, I was asked to write about my mother for a Mother's Day program at church. This is what I wrote:

Mother's Hands

While I was growing up, Mother's hands were always there, every step of the way, helping to mold her family's future. Now that I'm grown and raising my own family, I have an even deeper respect and appreciation for the guidance and sacrifices that she and my father made for us.

Mother's helpful hand was surely always there even before I can remember as an infant, and then her steady and disciplined hand was there in my adolescent years. Her guiding hand toward music and church was always present. (Going to church was never an option, you know!)

Mother taught the Adult Sunday School class for years and was the church organist and choir director for over twenty-five years.

Hers were also the hands of a den mother encouraging Scouting, of a committed parent and class sponsor, and of support and applause as a loyal fan who never missed a school or sporting event from Little League to junior high school, high school, and through my college football years.

My mother was so into her four kids and their sports that she hardly ever missed a sporting event that any one of us was involved in. Baseball, basketball, football—she was always there. She enjoyed the sports, beyond just wanting to support her kids. She'd sit in the stands at the baseball games with her scorebook, and she knew how to enter the symbols for strikeouts and balls and so on.

And then there was the supporting hand that was here to pick me up when I slipped or fell. The leading hand was also there teaching me to excel and never be satisfied with mediocrity or a follower's role.

Throughout her life, Mother always had both hands and arms outstretched and encompassing her family and friends. Here's a photo of Mother in a church presentation, with my daughter Sarah at her side.

Growing Up

My brothers and sister and I grew up at 801 North Magnolia, the house that Elisha and Irene Norvell had given to my grandparents, S.F and Irene Jackson, as a wedding present in 1914. In the 1950s, my parents put in a floor furnace, a welcome addition.

When I visit that house now, I wonder how in the world we all lived there. Mary Lucille had a large room across the back of the house, with seven windows, but my two brothers and I shared a tiny room with bunk beds. We had to go through Mary Lucille's room to get to one of the bathrooms, and she always wanted to charge us twenty-five cents for the privilege.

When she went off to college, N.F. got her room, and then I did. Bobby likes to point out that he only got it for one year, since he was so close to me in age.

Everything was nearby! Our school was half a block away, and the church two blocks. The Scout Hut was a half-block the other way. The Little League Field was only four blocks away.

When I was in the first grade, our teacher Miss Leonard had us put our beach towels on the floor between the desks and take a nap every day after lunch. That was back in the days when we were all afraid of Russia, so we also had bomb drills and practiced huddling under our desks.

In the third grade, I got in trouble for the first time in my school life. When the other kids went out to recess, Eddie Lee and I decided to stay in the classroom and throw a football around. We got caught and were sent to the office, where we got licks from Mr. Albert Griffith, the principal.

I remember, like it was yesterday, going home after school. As I was coming through the back yard, I saw my mother on the steps, waiting for me. Mr. Griffith had called my mother to tell her what had happened. I was surprised by that, and more surprised that the licking I got at school was nothing compared to the one I got at home!

My mother spanked me with the back of her hairbrush. It hurt. But I didn't throw footballs around the classroom ever again. I think that may have been the only time I ever went to a school office for punishment.

Mother was the disciplinarian in our family, because Daddy was always working. But when Daddy did punish us, which was very, very seldom, we remembered it.

There was a little shed next to our garage, and after N.F. hung palm fronds on it, we called it the Palm Hut. Since it was only seven or eight feet high, we liked to get up on the roof, but Daddy worried that we'd fall. He warned us not to get up there. Well, we did it anyway, and I'll never forget the licking we got for it. As I recall, that was the only time he ever had to spank us, but, man, it was a good one! His hands were large and calloused and they hit hard. Bobby said that Daddy only spanked us because Mother told him to. He didn't want to do it, but he did because the thought of us being on that roof scared him. He didn't want us to be hurt.

Growing up in the Jackson family included active participation in the First Presbyterian Church. For as long as we have had our own family, we have had our church family too. Our Presbyterian heritage began in Scotland, before being transplanted to a colony in Virginia. My great-grandparents, Elisha and Irene Norvell, brought that heritage to Rockport, and a plaque honoring them hangs above the door in one of the rooms of our church.

Sunday School, worship, youth group, and such were simply a part of our family's life. We never thought about *not* going. It was part of our routine, and it helped me become a well-rounded person with a strong faith at the center of my being. Church has been so much a part of my life that I cannot even imagine not being a part of the mission of the church.

The First Presbyterian Church is only two blocks south of the house where I grew up. Our congregation has benefitted from a lot of stability and longevity, compared to many churches which seem to change leadership frequently. I'm 60 years old, and we have had only four pastors in my lifetime.

Mother had us singing in her church choir as early as Junior High, and I also played the trumpet in band at school. Even though I was a six-sport letterman in high school athletics, I never gave up my place in the band. That's really difficult to do nowadays, but I'm very glad that being in a small school meant that I could do it. And I still sing in the church choir to this day.

Like our parents and grandparents before us, my brother Bobby and I have participated in many ways in the life and work of this church through the years. It is very much a big part of who I am. I only hope and pray that our kids and grandkids will follow this path as well.

My brothers, sister and I were four of thirty-one first cousins, including not just the Jackson family, but my mother's side too. Our family get-togethers could be huge, when everyone on the Jackson side gathered at our grandparents' 701 North Magnolia home at Christmas, and for Easter egg hunts.

The 17 Jackson first-cousins at S.F. Jackson home

My mother's parents lived in Austin. Grandmother Porter, named Neva (and Mother was named for her), was "Mom" to us. Our grandfather Porter, "Poppy," was a fantastic fisherman. When he came to visit, he and I would sometimes go fishing at Frandolig Island, which later became Key Allegro. Or at night, we might go down to the docks. We could catch thirty to fifty fish under the lights—big old reds, trout, drum. Other people might go with a guide and fish all over the bay, but then they'd come back and fish the shipyard piers—as we did—and get a full stringer.

Texas Parks and Wildlife sets limits now, but back then it was easy to catch a string of fish right there. The harbor had been fairly recently dredged, and there was no pollution or silting.

Rockport had only a couple of doctors at the time—L.G. Wood and not long after that, Homer Elliott.

I was the first kid in the neighborhood to drive, so I picked up everybody— Margie McNorton, my cousin Freddy Jackson, and Deborah McLead across the street from her, and Bobby of course. It was just a tight "old-Rockport" neighborhood.

Bobby and I were all into baseball. I made Little League All Stars three years, playing mostly in-field positions—first base, in this high school photo (top left next page).

I was a sports nut, in terms of participation. I played football, basketball, tennis, baseball, and track. In my twenties, I finally took up golf, but that's one sport I never took the time to master. I've always had such a dominant right arm, and that's a curse in golf.

The one sport that I carried the longest was football. I was made quarterback in the seventh grade and continued in that position all the way through twelfth grade.

I was privileged to play under some great coaches in all those years, and I had some good people in my backfield who went on to play college ball. Our team was definitely competitive, but overall our high school team was pretty mediocre in my senior year. I started on offense in high school, and played defense too,

since it was common to play both ways. I look back fondly on those days, recalling what I learned about teamwork, discipline, and hard work. And the year after I left, the high school team went on to win District. That happened to me again, after finishing up at college five years later.

My high school coach, Benny Bloomer, had played for the Javelinas of Texas A&I (now Texas A&M Kingsville) many years before, and I wanted to do that too. In the spring of my senior year in high school, while the Javelinas were in spring drills, Coach Bloomer took me to A&I and introduced me to the coach, Gil Steinke.

At A&I, a throwing quarterback was clearly a strength and a necessity in the late 1960s. Since I was more of a running quarterback, I really didn't expect to compete for the Quarterback position at A&I—not against passers from Houston, and such, who were all All-State and All-American players, and went on to play in the NFL.

But Coach Steinke knew that while I wasn't that fast, I was successful. When I graduated from Rockport-Fulton High School in 1969, he gave me my chance to play for the Javelinas, offering a small scholarship to Texas A&I. It just covered my books, tuition, and fees, but that was a start, and after playing one year as tight end, I got a half scholarship and then a full scholarship, starting as defensive end for three years.

During my senior year in high school, I was also fortunate enough to compete academically for a business scholarship offered by Central Power and Light Company. I won a $2400 scholarship—$600 per year for four years. That went a long way. In fact, for a good part of the time that I was in college, I could put that CP&L check in my pocket and use it for "whatever." My parents didn't have to pay anything for my college education, because of the football and academic scholarships.

I happened to be in college during the height of the Viet Nam war, so naturally I had a student deferment the whole time and when lottery came up, I had #243. Sometimes people ask me if I ever served in the military or went to Viet Nam, and my usual pat answer has been, "No, I did my Viet Nam during two-a-days in August in Kingsville, Texas, playing for Gil Steinke!"

Of course, I said that only in jest, meaning no disrespect for those who actually served in the military. I simply wanted to convey how tough it was with those two-a-days. When we reported each August, we had to go around the stadium—a two mile run—within a certain time, or we'd have to do it again.

Since I was not suited for the passing game at quarterback, I did time as tight end during my freshman year at A&I. Our talented team had significant depth that year, so the twenty or so freshmen had little chance to play. Only four of them made the traveling squad, and the rest of us got red-shirted. We watched from the sidelines as the Javelinas won a National Football Championship in 1969.

In my sophomore year, 1970, I played back-up tight end, and we won the National Championship again. I'll never forget that year, and the chance to win a National Champion football ring to commemorate it.

In the spring following that season, I got the chance to try my hand at defensive end. I loved it. Instead of being the one getting hit, I was the one inflicting the punishment. I was small, relative to the big offensive tackles and tight ends that I lined up against, but I learned how to read the opposing players and to use techniques which overcame my size difference. I became one of the starting defensive ends in the next season, 1971, and wound up starting there for three years.

Since I had been red-shirted in my freshman year, I saw the opportunity to play out my fifth year of collegiate football eligibility. I really wanted to do that, so in 1972, I purposely kept myself one course shy of graduating with my BBA and played my fifth year while working on my MBA.

Being on a national powerhouse team for those years was definitely an experience. My most prominent memories are simply of a lot of hard work under the direction of a demanding—and sometimes intimidating—coach. But that grueling experience generally kept me disciplined and focused. I managed to keep my grades up, and in fact made the All Lone Star Conference Academic Football Team in 1972 and the Academic All American Team in 1973.

As it turned out, though, that year was a book-end season—two and eight—a disaster for the team. We won our first and last games and lost all the ones in between, usually by only 2-4 points.

Every former athlete will tell you they always remember their last game, and mine was a 49-10 romp against our conference rival, Southwest Texas State. It was a great way to end my college football career.

And it was the first game of a forty-five game winning streak for A&I. The team won three consecutive national football championships in 1974, 1975, and 1976. So once again, after I left, the team went undefeated. I laugh about that unfortunate fact now.

Another highlight in the later years of my college career was the opportunity to pledge Sigma Chi fraternity in my junior year. My younger brother Bobby was already a Sig, and when I pledged in the spring of 1972, he was my Magister (pledge trainer).

Imagine that! My little brother could have made it "payback time" for me, but he didn't; Bobby and I actually became even closer through that time together. And I believe that the training/teaching experience actually got him started on becoming who he is today, a renowned teacher of Texas history with a flair for acting and performing.

I made lifelong friends in Sigma Chi, as I had through my football experience. My brothers in the fraternity were like another family, and many of us still get together from time to time.

Then I entered graduate school and stuck around until 1974, graduating with an MBA also. I would not trade anything in the world for all the great memories I had at Texas A&I.

During all the summers from 1965 to 1972, I worked at the Scout camp. And I ran up and down the camp, trying to get in shape for fall football. I had to leave the summer Scout camp in mid-August to go to "Two a Days" at A&I, and I had to show up in shape and ready to run.

I met Darla Rae Dobie while working at the Boy Scout camp following my junior year in high school. She was a couple of years younger than I, and she lived in Mathis, where the camp is located, so we began to date.

We got married when she was only eighteen and I was only twenty years old. At that age, you couldn't tell me anything; I knew it all. The marriage didn't last, but I spent more than half my college career married.

While I was in graduate school, I got a wild hair, yearning to fly. There was a little crop-duster strip in nearby Bishop, Texas, and Kenneth Theiss, who worked at Celanese, taught flying lessons there, after hours. In just one summer, I got my license. The plan was to come home and use this pilot's license in the business. Little did I imagine, then, how much my life was going to change.

Darla and I moved home from A&I in 1974, and in 1975 we started having serious marital issues. After a period of agony, trying to decide what to do, I finally told her, "I've had enough. I'm filing for divorce." It was pretty simple, since we had no children, no money, and no assets to split up. I haven't seen her since that day.

In my mind, I was divorced the day I filed for divorce; I had already tried everything I could. The marriage was over, and I was starting over. I decided to go to Corpus Christi that afternoon and commiserate with some buddies of mine. We met at Cantina Santa Fe, near Gaslight Square.

We started drinking at about 4:00 in the afternoon. Several hours later, my good friend Kerry said, "Let's go to King's Inn for dinner." Then he came up with a second idea: "Why don't I get you a blind date with Debbie Carlisle? She's a good friend of my wife, and lives near our apartment complex." By this time, I was pretty bleary-eyed from all the drinking, but I agreed.

When we picked up Debbie, eight people crowded into Kerry's big LTD car, heading for Kingsville. It was "dark-thirty" by then, and we were all past the point of driving responsibly. I was "feeling no pain," and although I had never smoked before in my life, I smoked that night.

We didn't get more than five miles out of Corpus before the car overheated. We turned around and came back and never got a thing to eat; we just went straight to another nightclub, Knight's Inn.

It was kind of a discotheque place, and we danced. And we never stopped drinking. Waves of nausea forced me to excuse myself and leave the room a time or two. I couldn't have made a good impression on Debbie.

Of course, I was hung over the next day. I felt horrible about all that had happened. In the afternoon, after the worst of my hangover subsided, I called Debbie on the phone. I apologized to her for the way I had acted and behaved, and asked her to give me another chance. She went out with me again, and I've never again been like I was the night of our first date.

During our courtship, I was concerned that people might think that Debbie was "the other woman." She wasn't! In my mind, my marriage was over before I met her. It was only coincidental that I met my future wife on the day that I filed for divorce from my first one. We dated incognito, not showing our faces in Rockport.

One of Debbie's cousins, who had been my fraternity brother in college, advised her not to marry me. He believed it would be a marriage on the rebound.

Well, eight months after we met, we did get married—on July 23, 1976, in Alice, Texas, and we've been married thirty-five years now (in 2011). Every time we see her cousins at a holiday gathering, we remind them of their discouraging and very inaccurate advice.

A Family of My Own

Debbie and I adopted our two children: Sarah in 1981 and Collin in 1985. We awaited their arrival as eagerly as any natural parent, and that baby girl and baby boy have been our kids from Day One. We don't think of them as adopted—except for a keen awareness and gratitude for the special relationships we have with them. We're so happy that we chose these children as a part of our family.

Too often, though, the demands of our seafood business forced me to spend up to eighty hours a week at work. Debbie bore the burden of being both mom

Sarah

Collin

and dad to our children some of the time, along with being a full-time teacher. We managed, but I sorely regret not being with my kids more, during their early, impressionable years. The first three or four years are crucial, and frequently, I was gone. I'll never get those years back.

Debbie and I had our struggles with parenting, as every couple does, but both Sarah and Collin have turned out fine. Collin has an amazing self-taught intellect in technology, particularly in the field of network assurance and internet security. He finished college in 2010 and has a bright future ahead of him.

Sarah, who is also college-educated, is now married to Kyle Wundt. They have given Debbie and me two beautiful grandchildren—Jackson Hays Wundt and Ainsley Estelle Wundt.

A "Stand by Your Man" Woman
Debbie Carlisle Jackson's Story

I had a blind date with Johnny on the day he filed for divorce from Darla. I thought, "Oh, well, nothing is going to come of this." He drank more heavily that night than I've ever seen him drink since. In all the years we've been together, there has been maybe one other time when he drank heavily, but I've never seen him the way he was on the night of our first date. He's always in control of his actions.

The day after we met, Johnny called and apologized for his behavior. He said, "Will you go out with me again?" I agreed, and we went to a football game that launched a whirlwind courtship. Within eight months we were married. Friends cautioned us against it then, and now Johnny likes to joke that it has now been a thirty-five-year rebound.

One of the things that I most admire in Johnny is that he never gives up; he never quits. He has a focus, and when he makes a plan, he follows it through. He gets a lot accomplished in a very short period of time. That's the way Johnny is; he's just a very Alpha Male. He's very dedicated to whatever he's doing—family, business, church, everything—and he follows through.

I saw that in Johnny during our whirlwind courtship. After my mother had Johnny researched, she and my father teased me that maybe I wasn't good enough for him! Johnny was dedicated to going to church, for example. I thought that was good, because I had dated a lot of people who didn't go to church much. Johnny had a plan—I could sense that. He had a plan for his life, what he wanted.

I think he has always been that way. When we went to one of his high school reunions, I saw in his yearbook that he was listed as "Most Dependable" or something like that. And it's true that you *can* depend on Johnny to do whatever you ask of him. He'll have it done within the hour, if that's possible.

With Johnny, I've always thought of myself as a "Stand by Your Man" kind of woman. I have stood by Johnny through thick and thin, because when things are bad, he always says, "We'll make it through this. We can get through it." And you know—we do. We *have*! We've gotten through a lot.

Right after we got married, I started teaching school here in Rockport, and of course Johnny was in the shrimping business. That was pretty rough work in the summer, and we never got a vacation. When most people were having fun, we couldn't do anything. Johnny worked every night until the shrimp boats were in, late, late at night. It was a tough job for him—a lot of physical hard work—that a shiny new MBA hadn't prepared him for.

And working with family was sometimes frustrating. Our parents were of the generation that didn't think anybody could do anything better than they could, and Johnny and his dad locked horns a lot. A couple of times, Johnny came home from work in the middle of the day, saying, "I quit. I can't work with that man." I didn't worry about it, because I knew he'd never quit for sure. And after a while, Johnny would cool down a little bit. I don't know if he and his dad ever apologized to each other, but they'd always get back together.

The shrimping business was up and down, up and down. And during that time, off and on for about five years, Johnny and I tried to have children. Then the shrimping business got really bad, and in 1979, Johnny and his dad started the Virginia scalloping venture. The next year, Johnny and I started working on an adoption. I stopped teaching and stayed home—in our beautiful new home in Harbor Oaks.

Not long after Sarah was born in May of 1981, Johnny went to Colombia with the shrimp boats. And four years later, we adopted a baby boy, naming him Collin, for my older brother who died in a car wreck when he was 19.

We had a lot of stress in the years that followed—the Chapter 11, the Aransas County Navigation District lawsuit. Then, in 1987, Johnny and his dad started the Florida scalloping venture. They alternated going back and forth to Florida. Sarah was six years old, and Collin was two. That was rough. Johnny was gone a lot, away from the house. Since his parents lived a few blocks away, on Cochran Lane in Little Bay Shores, Johnny's mother helped me with the kids. We just kept going.

We did what we had to do. We were so busy that there wasn't time to figure out which way we were going. We learned to take life day by day. We just had to figure out what the next day was going to be. I was working most of the time—teaching school—and I had most of the responsibility for the kids. We just had to keep going. We couldn't stop.

I think we suppressed a lot of frustration during that time; I know I did. And I think Johnny blamed himself, or felt guilty, because he wasn't home a lot when Collin was little. He couldn't be the driving force there, and Collin was a ring-tailed tooter while he was growing up. Our little boy was *all* boy, and very defiant. He never really got in trouble, but he just *did* things.

And Johnny and I kept going. We have a very good relationship. We can talk things through, to keep things on track. Of course, sometimes we get very frustrated at each other too; we do argue.

No marriage is perfect, but I've always felt very secure with Johnny. I come from a very family-oriented background and was brought up to understand that family comes first. Johnny is that way too. He does everything for everybody in our family. He takes care of everybody—his sister and his brother, as well as us. We do what we can to keep the family together. When things get tough, we work together. We have responsibilities to our children, and to working; we just keep doing what we do.

We've been through tough times, but mostly I think about the fun times. Johnny and I enjoy being around each other, and we like to have fun. We always make time for each other—to go and do things together. When we had kids at home, it was hard to go out alone, so we did things with the kids.

Johnny likes to go out probably more than I do. He'll go to every function there is in town, to be social. We like to dance—or we did when we were younger, before my knee got bad. (I finally got it fixed in January 2011.) We make sure we do something on the weekend, to go out together. We like to go on little trips, and now we go to the ranch on weekends a lot.

We have a lot of friends, and I think that network is really important. That's what keeps people together. We run with couples, basically, who have been married a long time. Some have had problems over the years, but we try to surround ourselves with people who are pretty stable in their marriages, as we are in ours.

Johnny and I believe it's important for us to be around stable people like that, and for our kids to be around them too. We discuss that a lot.

Last year, we were in Galveston over Memorial Day, with a group of our friends. One of the couples was celebrating their fortieth wedding anniversary. One of the husbands who was there has had four open-heart surgeries, and he's

Our ranch cabin 2010

only sixty-one years old. He has a bucket list, and he came to me and said, "One of the items on my list is to go on a boat trip with you and your husband."

Right away, I answered, "When do you want to go?" We've planned the cruise for this summer—aboard a fifty-six-foot catamaran with a crew. We're all looking forward to that dream get-away.

I'm always trying to get Johnny away from his office. Before we had the ranch, he was at the office Saturdays and Sundays. Now, the minute we get back from the ranch on Sunday, he's there. I tell him now he should work only four days a week, but he just shakes his head.

Our kids are wonderful. We don't even think about the fact that they're adopted. Sarah was pretty easy. She was a typical girl, with a lot of drama, but she's very caring and giving. When she graduated from high school, she joined "Up with People," but the program phased out when she was just half way through her year. They were going to give her college credit, but she found only three schools in the nation that would accept those credits. One of them was in Hawaii, so guess where she decided to go? Sarah moved way over there to Honolulu in January, 2001.

In July of that year, we went to Hawaii to visit Sarah, and while we were there, Johnny and I renewed our marriage vows on Maui. We took seven of our friends with us.

Sarah completed her spring and fall semesters in Hawaii, but then 9/11 hit. There are so many military bases on Oahu and Sarah said that all the alarms were sounding and they feared it would be Pearl Harbor all over again. Since she lived near Pearl Harbor, she was terrified. Sarah wanted to come home, but she couldn't get out. Johnny told her, "You stay right where you are, and as soon as we can, we'll get you out of there." I think he was scared, too.

Sarah came home and went to UTSA. She got a degree in Criminal Justice, and went to her first job in Tyler, with Child Protective Services. Sarah couldn't handle what she was seeing; she had too big a heart. Mostly, I think she missed her boyfriend Kyle Wundt.

She moved to San Marcos that summer and went back to school at Texas State (which was formerly SWT). There she got her teaching certificate, but never used it. She and Kyle got married just weeks after her graduation.

Two months after the wedding, Sarah was pregnant. She's a stay-at-home mom, and a great mother to Jack and to Ainsley. The family enjoys a really good life on their ranch at Belmont, Texas.

Our son Collin has a big heart, just as Sarah does; both our kids are very sensitive that way. But Collin was a stinker growing up. His little mind just worked unbelievably. He was so smart when he was little, as much as he is now.

When he was about eight years old, I came home from running errands and saw the Aransas Natural Gas Company truck parked at our house. A man stood outside it, shaking his head. He said to me, "I don't know how your boy knew who to call, but there's a gas leak here." Collin had originally looked in the phone book and called an oil and gas company in Portland, not a residential gas provider. The man who ultimately came to our house told me, "I've got men working for me who don't know what to do, but your son knew how to shut the gas off. It's just amazing what this boy knows."

Another time, he devised this "construction" of heavy plastic and duct tape and kept it inflated with a fan. It was a sort of 'hideout' for him and his friends, on our deck above the garage.

Collin has always been inquisitive like that. But while he was growing up, he wanted everything his way, because he believed that was the *right* way. He didn't want to have to study anything that didn't pertain directly to what he wanted to do once he graduated. And he was still like that, in college.

He's an I-T guy for the County now. He has turned out to be a very dependable, settled-down young man. We get compliments all the time about what a nice young man he is. He's my kid, and sometimes I wonder, "When did this happen?"

As I've indicated, both of our kids are adopted, and that has never mattered to them or to Johnny and me. Both adoptions were "closed," as was the practice

then, but now, some people have open adoptions. I don't know; I'm not sure which way is the best.

One day fairly recently, when Sarah and I were out together and talking about one thing and another, she said, "You know, I've often thought about trying to find my birth mother."

"Well," I said, "if you want to, we can do that."

"I know it's not going to be what I expect," Sarah said.

"It may not be," I agreed. "And you also have to consider what your birth mother wants."

"I know, I know. It would be kinda awkward to see her, but I'm just curious."

I said, "I'm curious, too. If you ever want to do that, we will help you."

Lately, Sarah has had some health issues that may have a genetic connection, so we may all find there's another reason for locating her birth mother.

Collin never would say much about being adopted, though he'd get mad sometimes and say, "You're not my real mother!"

I think he was just trying to hurt my feelings, so I'd answer, "Oh, but I *am* your real mother."

And after that talk with Sarah, I told him, "If you ever want to find out about your birth parents, we can help you. "

He didn't have a response, but I know that once adopted kids are out of school and becoming adults, they start wondering. ❧

TAKING THE TIDE

PART IV

MISERIES

Fires

Fires have marked our family. Just before my great-grandparents arrived in Rockport, the town acquired a fire wagon with a chemical tank and a large black horse to pull it. When a fire alarm came in, volunteers might hitch the horse to that wagon, or they might just tie a rope to it and pull it with their saddle horses.

The arrangement was a good start, but hardly enough protection. Six years later, my great-grandmother wrote:

> We had a very gloomy winter caused by so many fires. We had a building boom that collapsed, and it is thought the fires were not legitimate, but for insurance.
>
> The first originated in a saloon in the middle of the business block facing west. It swept right up the street, destroying all in the path, including Sorenson's two-story brick store. Two nights after that, a two-story residence across the street from our home burned in the night, destroying the home next to it. As the wind was due west, it seemed for a time we could not save our place. Mama and I threw sheets on the floor and piled clothes in them to tie up and carry out.
>
> Irene was a little thing and so frightened she impeded my movements by clinging to my skirts. I told her to go save something. The laundry had

Sorenson's two-story brick store

just come in, and I placed it on the sheet, so Irene got the wet soap off the work stand and threw it on the fresh clothes, saying, "I'll save that." Then she thought of her little pink parasol of which she was so proud, and added it to the pile.

I shall never forget how we suffered from thirst. As our throats became parched, we had to take the precious time to go for a drink.

The fires went on in different parts of the town until it was rumored there was a combined effort to burn Rockport. A watch patrol was organized, the men in their block taking turns watching each night. Mama and I did not take off our clothing for five nights in succession, and we kept our trunks packed and stationed by an outside door all winter. We had one big fire insurance trial, but of course no proof could be obtained.

1938

Rockport's city fire department was inactive after The Great Depression, but we could have used it when a fire swept through some apartments in June. The town's equipment was no match for the fire; only a change of wind saved the town. Then the Aransas Pass Fire Department came in to extinguish the blaze.

In response to the disaster, a group of citizens formed the Aransas County Emergency Corps. Its mission was to protect lives and property in emergencies such as hurricanes, tornadoes and fires. My dad served as an Assistant Fire Chief.

The 1960s

On a warm night in 1962, I was in the school auditorium watching my brother N.F. in a high school play. We didn't have air conditioning, and the windows were open so the breeze could come in.

N.F. was on stage, wearing a white tuxedo, sitting with his stage girlfriend Becky Rouquette. My brother Bobby recalls that N.F. was about to kiss Becky . . . when suddenly there was an explosion. The window rattled at the school, and we saw a flash of light, illuminating the whole night sky.

We heard people yelling, "It's Jackson's!" They came up to the windows, shouting. "There's a fire at Jackson's!" We could see the red and yellow glow in the sky as we got up and left the auditorium. And of course school officials called off the play.

N.F. had his driver's license, so there he was, in his white tuxedo, getting in his car to take us to the harbor. Soon we could see that the fire was at the shipyard that we leased from Rob Roy Rice. Hundreds of people, from all over town, milled around. Although no one was allowed closer than a block or so from the fire, we were in the fire zone. N.F's white jacket turned dark with ash.

Flames shot one hundred feet into the air, engulfing the four-story wood-framed building that Rice had used, and maybe Westergard before him. Fire departments from the entire area battled the blaze, and we could do nothing but watch as the building went down. That huge building and everything in it was a hopeless loss.

Bobby recalls: "As youngsters, the only thing my brothers and I could think about was the brand new motorboat—a ski boat—that Gene Carter had been building there for us. Gene, who was Daddy's friend as well as a carpenter working for him, had almost finished the boat. Just the night before, we had watched him put the motor on it. We were planning to take it out that weekend and launch it."

Just one year later, on August 28, 1963, fire struck again. This time it was at Morrison's Boathouses—on property he leased from us. The tin-roofed boat house, built out over the water, accommodated yachts forty to fifty feet long. I'll never forget seeing all those fine yachts getting burned.

The volunteer fire department came with their trucks and equipment. My dad had always been a member of the department, but this time it was his own place that was burning.

Mother was frantically trying to find Daddy. When she finally saw him, he was right in the middle of the action—as usual. Mother was begging him, "Norvell, don't go in there!" but Daddy went into the boathouse inferno.

His best friend, Floyd Smith, had a boat there, *Breakaway*, that he ran for someone. It was a really nice, big yacht—one of the finest in Rockport at that time. Daddy risked his life inside the burning boathouse to try to free up *Breakaway*. He thought that if he could get her loose, and push her out into the harbor, she wouldn't burn.

All of us watched Daddy on that boat and others, trying to take the lines off, single-handedly moving boats around the harbor to get them away from the fire, catching a burning hull as it floated across the Fish Bowl. He saved several boats, I think.

When Daddy came back to us, covered with smoke, Mother went and hugged him. Then, sobbing, she asked, 'What are we going to do?'

In the light of the flames, Daddy chuckled, 'Well, honey, we'll just start over.'

The next day, our fire made the front page of the *Corpus Christi Caller-Times* newspaper. A headline read: *12 Yachts Destroyed in Blaze at Rockport*. The article declared those yachts among the "finest in South Texas," and reported estimated losses at $500,000.

The fire burned for days. There was a suspicion of arson, but no one officially determined the cause.

We did start over. But there was another fire in those boathouses in 1966. Our *Rockport Pilot* newspaper headlined it a "$125,000 fire," with nine yachts destroyed or extensively damaged. Daddy believed the fire had started on one of two boats, since he saw them blazing when he arrived. Although the fire raged for three hours, Daddy told the *Pilot* that the firemen "did a terrific job in preventing the fire from destroying all sixteen of our boat stalls."

The fire department again suspected that someone had set fire to the boathouses. Vandals and drunks used the boat houses as a place to sleep. Maybe someone threw a cigarette where a whiskey bottle had spilled. Or it could have been arson: someone mad at someone else, and wanting to get even.

It seemed strange that we had three significant fires in five years—big fires, for Rockport—but I guess we'll never know what caused them.

Hurricanes

Great-grandmother Irene Norvell wrote in her memoir, 1919: *We had the warning of a tropical hurricane, then it did not materialize, and we heard nothing of it for a week, though there was a high tide.*

A sailor in the crow's nest of a ship had seen the rain bands. Noting the wave caps and the flutter of the flags, he estimated the wind at thirty-nine miles per hour. The purser signaled it to other ships by light and flag; vessels nearest land telegraphed the word: tropical storm. That's when Rockport received its first warning.

The tropical storm continued westward, slipping between Puerto Rico and Haiti. It slammed into the Florida Keys and dallied there for three days before finally passing south of Key West. The *Corpus Christi Caller* headline read: "South Florida Prostrated by Gale; Property Loss Appalling." People in Rockport figured the end of the storm was in sight, but it kept moving across the Gulf of Mexico. Then people speculated it would blow ashore in Louisiana.

On September 12, the Weather Bureau in Washington, D.C. issued a clear warning: "This is the worst hurricane in history." Most people in Rockport paid little attention; weather warnings were a dime a dozen each September. They still believed the storm had gone ashore in Florida.

But by Saturday night, September 13, my great grandmother, along with everyone else, knew better. She wrote:

The night was quite stormy, so in the morning we did not hurry to get up. We knew we could not have Sunday School or Church. Mr. Norvell, as soon as he was dressed, said he would go down and see about the water. He came back with an excited look on his face and said he was appalled at the bay.

Then I said I would go have a look. When I came back, I said, "I am not going to stay here a minute."

"Oh, go on, don't be a quitter. Get breakfast, and then I will get a car and send you to Irene's."

My reply was, "What do I care about breakfast. I can get that at Irene's."

That was the dialogue between us, but of course I went to the kitchen and hastily prepared the meal.

Then Mr. Norvell left and went to look after the Lightburne sisters, who were spinsters. While he was gone, the blind blew open on the north east window of the living room. It was with great difficulty that I could pull it in, only to find that the catch had broken.

Nana's previous experiences in the 1916 storm dictated her preparations this time around.

I did not know what to do, then I noticed just in reach of my hand there hung on the wall a calendar having a heavy silk cord. With my free hand and my teeth I managed to loosen it, and tie the blinds together. Then I covered up the piano and got together some silver and other valuables.

By that time, Mr. Norvell returned and said he could find no car that the owner would risk making the trip. He said there was no use to talk of walking, because he had to bend almost double.

I said, "We can go on Dick." [Dick was the name of their horse.] *He made no objection and in a few minutes we were mounted, I riding man-fashion behind him. I could not have stayed on any other way.*

There was no water in the town then, but the wind was so strong that the rain would sting so, and we had to keep our heads down. The wind would sometimes strike Dick broadside with such force that he would be driven across the road. Then again it would strike him full in the face, and he would turn around like a top.

When we reached the [railroad] *station, still keeping our heads down, we did not see the wires that were hanging down till we ran against them. As soon as Mr. Norvell deposited me at Irene's, he went back to see about his Lightburne responsibility.*

He tried to persuade them to leave immediately, but they argued against it, showing him substantial kitchen shelves that reached almost to the ceiling, and were wide enough that they could climb up there. Finally he told them to come look at the breakers showing above the Ridge, and they then agreed, provided that he would read some scripture and pray.

I never heard that the scripture was read, and I imagine the prayer was a short one. He had planned to take one sister behind him on the horse, to the Traylor place, and then come back for the other. But so much time had been wasted that he could not risk it.

Mr. Norvell put both of the ladies on, and then he led the horse. From there he went to see about Judge and Mrs. Stevens [at Water and Hackberry streets]. *The Judge had refused to leave, so when Mrs. Stevens saw Mr. Norvell coming, she felt so relieved; she felt sure he could persuade her husband. But then she saw Mr. Norvell reach the little bridge, pause a little, then turn and go back.*

Mr. Norvell said Dick refused to go, so he thought it better not to force him. Afterwards, he found there was no bridge, and then he came on up to us [at 801 Magnolia]. *Ford* [S.F.] *came home before noon, leaving water in his office.*

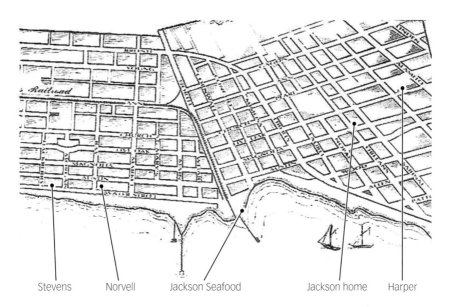

Stevens   Norvell   Jackson Seafood   Jackson home   Harper

The wind was increasing in intensity all the while, and we were so afraid that his big front window would blow in. I told him what we did in Goliad—nailed bed slats across the window—so we did that. While I was helping Ford, I glanced out the window and was startled to see water covering the road.

"Ford, is that the Bay?"

"Oh, no, I think not," he replied. But he made some excuse and left the room, then came back pretty soon. "It is the Bay," he said.

Then we got busy and worked fast, trying to make things as safe as possible. In the course of the preparation, Norvell began to jump up and down, crying joyfully, "The fitch tree is gone; the fitch tree is gone."

Rockport School
Courtesy of Kam Wagert,
from her postcard collection

My father, who was only four years old at the time, was trying to say "the switch tree." As my great-grandmother explained: *That it was a tree just across the road, to which Norvell's mother resorted when there was a naughty little boy who needed correction.*

At 4 o'clock, we were ready to leave the house. There was then 18 inches of water in the yard. We had decided to go to the school house. Mr. Norvell took the two boys on the horse, with Jim Bart crying all the way because the rain was stinging his face.

Irene and I were loaded down with some provisions and dry clothing. Ford, who had baby Isabel, picked up the big milk bucket and held it over her head. How he held it steady enough to prevent bumping her I don't know, but evidently he did, for when he relieved her of it she was smiling and in the best of good humor.

We went along with many others plodding through the water. Mr. Frank Sparks came riding up and said, "Don't go to the school house; the walls are falling." So we turned and went on up the road.

I was soon exhausted. I had on a heavy winter cloak that had gotten so wet that morning, and I was carrying so much. When we reached the house now owned by Mr. Harper, all the fences were gone, so Mr. Norvell turned his horse in there. He went round to the back of the house and we followed.

It was entirely occupied by men who worked at the ship yard, and took their meals elsewhere. They gave up their beds to us. Of course we sat up all night, but were glad to have the beds for the children.

There were about 50 refugees there and just once the water swept through the lower floor of house. Old Mr. Porter was brought there in a boat.

About midnight there was a terrific electric storm. Then the wind changed to the opposite direction, and early in the morning we went home on dry ground.

I was afterwards told the only funny thing that occurred in Rockport that day was the sight of me riding along Austin Street astride the horse.

But really it is thought that I saved some lives by so doing. At the Morris Hotel on the beach, I had a young music pupil who saw me and called her mother to look and she was laughing heartily at the ridiculous sight. But her mother took it seriously and said, "They have been here longer than we have and realize there is a danger. So we will get out too."

She tied a rope around her waist, and had all the children holding it, thus making a line of all of them. The wind was so strong they only managed to reach Austin Street, turn and take refuge upstairs in one of the business houses. In a few minutes, the Morris House was a mass of kindling wood.

It was Thursday before I could get down home. The town was under martial law, so I had to get a permit, and then there was so much broken glass in the streets that it was not safe.

Our house was not damaged a great deal. The northeast window in the living room had blown in, ruining my curtains and rug; the fences were down; and the chimneys were off even with the roof. Some chickens were saved by coming up on the back porch. The yard was a sight to behold: six boats, a piano and big timbers from the old Pavilion, and one tremendous trunk of a tree. One side of the lattice had blown in, the other out, but the front remained. Still, we could not get out that way for a long time because old logs and rubbish piled up there.

Mr. Norvell proposed we walk down the ridge a few blocks. Such wrecked homes and devastation everywhere! We had to walk very carefully, and would not go more than a few yards before coming across a dead rattlesnake. One I remember must have been quite ancient—it was so very large.

I think it was after this that I went over to see about my music room. I could not get to it sooner. I took a negro girl with me to clean up. We had so many things to contend with that followed the storm. That morning, I think I ran most of the way, as big mosquitoes would settle in quantities. They were a new variety, sluggish; I could brush them off, but they had a sting.

When I went inside the room, the first thing I did was to fall down. The floor was still wet and slimy, and there was salt water still standing on the Steinway piano, because there was a close wire netting at the back.

I did not go home to stay for quite a while, because there were repairs to be made and it was hard to procure help. I used to go down there when I wanted to be quiet and write letters. I would open the front door and sit there, and men would come riding on horses right up against the porch.

They had made a narrow path through there, as there was so much debris along the beach. It was five months before we could get all of that moved, so that we could put up the fence.

My grandfather's fish house—the business he had just bought from his brother—was gone. Many others were too. Few boats were intact; nets and seines were gone. My grandfather found his company's big iron safe down on Main Street.

He had to start over completely, when he had just assumed the obligation of paying off his brother Roy. So he had a double burden.

Although the fishing industry was paralyzed for some time, it is indicative of my grandfather's character and courage that he successfully paid off his financial losses and built a destroyed business into a successful one.

1961, Carla

Daddy never considered evacuating during a storm. The fish house was such a big part of his life that he just couldn't go off and leave it, but he made the rest of the family leave. He sent us off somewhere, north or south, depending on where the hurricane hit.

I was only ten when Hurricane Carla arrived on September 19. Mother took us to Alice before the storm, and we stayed in the Americana Motel there. I remember coming back and seeing rattlesnakes, and lots of boats in the streets, and power lines down, and trees in people's yards.

The entire Rockport School, just around the corner from our house, was full of National Guardsmen camping out on cots. I guess they had been put in Rockport to help keep peace. Carrying their rifles, they went up and down the beach, shooting rattlesnakes that came over from San Jose Island.

And I remember driving up Highway 35 to Port Lavaca, and seeing shrimp boats out in the fields.

1967, Beulah

This was the second tropical storm, second hurricane, and the only major hurricane during the 1967 storm season. Beginning on the afternoon of September 17, people were advised to remain off the beaches of Padre, Mustang, and San Jose islands. Two days later, people on the islands, and then in Rockport and on the Lamar Peninsula, got the word to evacuate. Daddy decided that I was old enough to stay for this one, but Bobby still had to leave to be with Mother.

The thing that was weird about Beulah was that it was a nighttime storm. Central Power and Light Company pulled all the power down—probably to keep electrical fires from occurring—so we had no light, anywhere. And of course, it was overcast, because of the storm; there were no stars, no moonlight. It was pitch black, and all that noise of wind and rain and unidentifiable things flying around.

I couldn't see my hand in front of my face; that's how black it was. I was sixteen, and wading around in thigh-deep water at Jackson Seafood. We had flashlights, of course, and went back and forth checking between the Quonset hut and the boat slips.

Around that same time, a house on Key Allegro caught fire, lighting up the dark sky with an unbelievable radiance.

I was walking along, between the ice vault and the boat houses that we had just rebuilt from the 1966 fire. Then, all of a sudden, the water went from thigh-deep to ankle-deep. In less than five minutes, the water just went out.

It was freaky! We had no idea what was going on. Then, about ten minutes later, the water came back up. Again, we had no clue. It just felt weird.

I didn't know what had happened until the next morning. That's when we found out that a tornado had gone through Fulton. It sucked all that water out. And of course when the tornado had passed, the water came back.

Daddy was on the City Council then, so on the day after the storm, I got to go the City Hall with him. We were working with Herman Johnson, the City Manager. Delmar Hiller was the Mayor, and he wanted to go in his open-top jeep to survey the damage. He let me ride with him, and we drove up to Fulton to see what had happened there.

A waterspout in the bay had come ashore as a tornado. In a hundred-yard-wide swath that went all the way through Fulton, we found nothing larger than matchstick-sized wood. All the buildings had just exploded, and the Casterline Fish Company had been at the center of that path.

The Sanchez and Benavidez homes, across 5th Street from Fulton Elementary

We drove to the Fulton Elementary School and found it untouched. But across the street, north of the school, we saw annihilation that I will never forget. On the corner across from the school, there was nothing left of the house where Buddy and Katherine McLester had lived.

From Fulton, the tornado had continued inland, across Highway 35. Nothing remained of a honky-tonk called Lillian's Danceland. We saw a few pieces of lumber back in the brush, but that was all.

Later, we learned what had happened to the McLesters' house. Before Hurricane Beulah hit, boat owners in Fulton moved their craft to the relative safety of bar ditches along the road. One man decided that the bar ditch by Constable Buddy McLester's house would be the safest place, and McLester agreed that he could put it there.

Buddy and his wife Katherine sat out the storm at the Sheriff's Office, but after it passed, Katherine wanted to go home. Buddy took her to their house at Fifth and Mesquite Streets in Fulton, then returned to his job, patrolling the streets.

Katherine took a bath and then got in bed with *Reader's Digest*. She heard a sound like a freight train, and something told her to get on the floor and put her head between her legs, so she did that. She felt the floor raise up; she heard glass breaking; she felt rain on her face. When things calmed down, she tried to move around, and felt the floor slippery beneath her. Katherine realized that she was on linoleum, and the only linoleum in her house was in the kitchen. She couldn't imagine how she'd got out the bedroom door, down the hall, and through the door into the kitchen.

Katherine saw a candle in a window at the Cookstons' house across the street, and walked over there. Pounding on the door, she called out, "Let me in! My house has blown away." She was scratched and bruised, and later a blood clot developed in her leg, from the pressure, but otherwise she was all right.

The McLester home had been thrown 50-60 feet from its foundation, and then exploded. Most of the house was leaning up against a tree; the only flat part was the section of kitchen linoleum floor that Katherine had found herself sitting on. And where the house had been, now lay, upside down, the boat that had carefully been placed in the bar ditch before Beulah came to visit.

Several days after the storm, Buddy McLester got a phone call from a man in Copano Cove. "I found your stepson's letterman's jacket from high school up in one of my trees," he said. The tornado's winds had carried the jacket that far, and it would have been lost forever, except that Tommy McCabe's name was embroidered inside the pocket.

Charlie Marshall, the funeral director, started calling Katherine McLester "Lucky" after her tornado experience. "Hey, there, Lucky!" he says when he sees her. Katherine shakes a finger at him. "You're not getting me today, Charlie," she always responds.

These days, Buddy and Katherine's son, Rick McLester, tells this story when he gives talks on hurricane preparedness. He adds that a professional photographer took more than a dozen photos of the house, but the family doesn't have them now. They lent the pictures to someone who never returned them.

Hurricane Beulah spawned hundreds of tornados, I think, and a lot of rain.

We had less wind than some storms bring, but more tide. Still, for me, what made Beulah so scary was that it was a night storm. We couldn't see anything.

1970, Celia

Celia arrived on August 3. She was a worse storm than Beulah many times over, but she was a daytime storm, so at least we could see what we were doing.

N.F. was away in the Navy and couldn't get home in time to help. Bobby and I were off working as Staff Members at the Boy Scout camp, but we came home.

Bobby insisted that Daddy wouldn't send him off this time. He said that he was old enough to stay and do what needed to be done. Daddy agreed to that, but he made all his employees go. "You take care of your families," he told them, "and you leave."

We started to work early in the morning, getting all the records out of the business offices, and the furniture and equipment up high. That took hours.

One of our jobs was to protect the boathouses since they were open to the wind. Their tin roof sat at an angle, so Daddy gave Bobby the job of nailing it down more securely. Then Daddy and I went out to tie our fleet of shrimp boats to the dock, loosening and retightening lines so that they could rise with the storm surge. Daddy speculated that if we got the tides that were forecast, the boats could get loose; lines would break and our boats would be found all over downtown Rockport when the storm was over. We jumped from boat to boat, adjusting the lines when we saw one getting loose.

We were still on the boats at 10:00 or 10:30 in the morning, re-tying boats and pumping them out, when the tide came. As the water rose over the bulkhead, I watched the lines tighten. The boats rose nearly to the top of the pilings, and I wondered what would was going to happen when there was no more piling left.

The wind was coming from the north, and strengthening. By mid-afternoon, it was fierce. Bobby climbed down the ladder at the boathouses and came looking for us. In those days, the fish house was an old World War II-type Quonset hut out on the point of our property. By the time Bobby found us, the tin had started coming off the rounded roof of the Quonset hut. Then the steel structural beams started to bend, turning it into a giant steel pretzel as the entire building came apart.

We took refuge behind the ice vault, huddling in the red panel truck and unable to see much of what was happening to Rockport. Downtown buildings were being destroyed. Debris flew everywhere. And the water was still rising.

The atmospheric pressure dropped. Our ears popped again and again, trying to adjust to the pressure. Then the back windshield of the truck exploded; it just

Boathouse   Quonset hut

Quonset hut
Photo courtesy of Nan Jackson

blew right out. Bobby was a basket case.

At that point, I realized for the first time that Daddy was afraid—not for his own safety, but for his two kids (I was 19 and Bobby was 18). He realized that if we stayed there much longer, the wind would come from the other direction and we wouldn't have the protection of the ice vault.

"We gotta get outta here," Daddy said. We needed to leave while we had the chance, and save our lives even if we couldn't save anything else.

Water was already getting into the truck. And we had another problem: All the tin that Bobby had been hammering down on the roofs of the boat houses had just peeled away like paper and was flying around us. Some settled to the ground and piled up, blocking our escape route.

Daddy thought for a minute and then said, "Johnny, you take the wheel. Drive slow."

He got out of the truck and walked ahead of us, removing debris so we wouldn't get a flat tire. Looking back on that, it was crazy; he could have been beheaded by tin sheets and debris flying at 150-200 miles an hour.

I can still see Daddy there, and I marvel that he managed not to be sliced up by those sharp edges. The 200-yard drive seemed to take "forever."

Without the ice vault providing us with a wind break, the side panel of the truck caught the full force of the wind. We could feel the windward wheels come slightly off the ground.

Entrance to Jackson Seafood

Old railroad tracks

Daddy's courageous effort did not prevent us from getting four flat tires, but he kept motioning me on. When we finally got to Max's Tackle Shop on Austin St., Daddy hopped in the truck, and we drove on the rims all the way to the sheriff's office, next to the Court House. We were scared, but we all got out safely. We spent the rest of the day and night with several others who found refuge at the sheriff's office.

The next day, we went to check on our property. The Quonset hut was gone; the office building inside it was gone; the boat barns were gone. There was virtually nothing left, but most of our boats were safe.

Our house on Magnolia was fine. A few trees got uprooted, and the house had some broken windows, but otherwise it was okay. We slept there, but for the next two or three days, we mostly lived where the fish house had been.

We had the only ice in town—thousands and thousands of tons of ice. It might take a couple of months for all that to melt, even without electricity to

My cousin, Nan Jackson, took this picture, and the similar one preceding it, after Celia. On the back of this one, she wrote: "What remains of the dry and wet stalls of Jackson Channel & Dock Co." (formerly Morrison's)

keep the plant running. Since that ice could provide the only potable water in town, we gave it, for free, to anyone who asked.

Hundreds of folks lined up with bowls and cooking pans and ice chests. After the storm, N.F. had managed to get from Puerto Rico to Rockport, so he helped us shovel ice. We shoveled in the vault with flashlights and lanterns—twenty-four/seven, it seemed, for a couple of days. What a relief it was when the Budweiser trucks rolled into town, loaded with thousands of beer cans filled with good water!

There was no electricity anywhere, no communications, so initially Mother, Mary Lucille, and N.F. had no idea that we were still alive. Reports on TV and radio said that Rockport had been 100% destroyed, that many people were missing or dead. Of course it was all exaggerated.

Bobby recalls: "Mother couldn't get back for three or four days. When she finally reached Rockport, she went straight to our house. Of course she arrived in the daytime, so she could see inside, even without electricity.

"We were down at the fish house, but Mother didn't know that. When she couldn't find us, she started screaming. She went into every single bedroom and saw, by every bed, a candle in a porcelain holder. When she saw those candles, she knew we were alive. She got on her knees, kissed the candles, and thanked the Lord. Then she came down to the fish house and found us all.

"Later, Mother put masking tape on each of those candles, marking them with our names and the name of the storm, 'Celia, 1970.' The candles were to her then, and to us now, a treasured symbol of life."

After Hurricane Celia, Daddy decided not to leave our boats at the dock during any more hurricanes. When boats get loose, they bang into each other, and they can even end up in downtown Rockport. After that, we started anchoring our boats in the bay. Later, when we had steel boats, that became even more important; those heavy boats could do a lot more damage.

We never did rebuild the Morrison boat sheds, destroyed in two fires and then again in Hurricane Celia.

I believed that things were finally on an even keel, at least on the personal front. It was some years before two more sad things happened in our family.

Bereavement

I suppose most people—especially if they come from loving families—feel that they lose their parents too soon. Certainly that's how I felt when my mother was diagnosed with esophageal cancer. It attached to her lungs and elsewhere, so the doctors felt they could do little for her. But Mother was a fighter. She lived the full six months that the doctors had predicted, and then six and a half years more.

Daddy cared for my mother daily during her long illness; he waited on her hand and foot. I would imagine she has a "to do" list for him still.

But by 1995, Daddy had signs of Alzheimer's, and from that point on Mother was taking care of Daddy as much as he took care of her. In the end, that proved too much for her. In 1997, she just gave up.

Daddy held on for another seven years. He had never been a quitter, always landed on his feet, so he fought death and stayed in control, as much as he could, right up to the end. He didn't eat for the last week or so of his life, but on the final day, he did eat lunch—and it was fish.

Daddy left a legacy of tireless energy and devotion, an indefatigable work ethic, civic responsibility, undying loyalty, and above all, Faith. ❧

TAKING THE TIDE

PART V
TAKING THE CURRENT

R ecently, an acquaintance told me that his work sends him into a lot of communities; he hears a lot of people speak. After he came to a couple of events here, he said to me, "The quality of people you have in Rockport is better than any I've ever seen. It's not like this everywhere else."

Unsolicited, he tells me this! And it makes my point: There's a gold mine of people here. I've worked with them in every one of my community-based ventures.

Scouting

My mother and dad had been very supportive of Scouting from the very beginning. First, my sister Mary Lucille was an active Girl Scout. When my elder brother, N.F., was ready for Cub Scouts, my mother volunteered to be his den mother, in Den Four. They met in our house, and soon both Mother and Daddy were convinced that Scouting was a great program.

Of course, Scouting didn't have a lot of competition in those days. We basically had Little League Baseball, Church, Scouts, and maybe a summer job. Nowadays, there are many activities competing for kids' time, and Scouting has taken a back seat to some of them.

Bobby and I followed N.F. into the program, and since we were just thirteen months apart in age, we were in the same den, meeting in our own home, with mother as our Den Mother. When we grew from Cub Scouts to Boy Scouts, our Troop 49 met less than a block away from our house. It was a neighborhood thing; we just went around the corner to our Scout meetings.

There were three sons in our family, and all three of us became Eagle Scouts. All three

of us were also in the Order of the
Arrow, which is another kind of honor
camping organization. And we were
all three Vigil Honor Members, the
highest honor a Scout can get in the
Order of the Arrow.

In 1964, I went to the National
Scout Jamboree in Valley Forge, Penn-
sylvania, and that was a pretty big deal
for me. We made a side trip to the New
York World's Fair and Washington,
D.C.

In about 1967, I was named Outstanding Eagle Scout of the Mustang
District, one of nine Texas districts in

1969

our Council. The Outstanding Eagles from all those districts were invited to the
State Capitol to meet with the Governor, and my dad went along as a chaperone.

As we were coming down the rotunda of the Capitol, from way across the
other side, Governor John Connally recognized my dad from the days when they
had been fraternity brothers at the University of Texas.

They hadn't seen each other in some thirty years, but Connally called out,
"Hey, Iron Head!" I felt my jaw drop. And when John Connally wrote his auto-
biography, he actually referred to my dad as Iron Head, the nickname Daddy got
at Shreiner College. It meant a lot to me, that Governor Connally remembered
Daddy's nickname after all those years.

Governor John Connally, fifth from left, Johnny Jackson, sixth from left,
and Norvell Jackson, far right

(As you may know, after serving as the 39th Governor of the State of Texas, Connally went on to become the U.S. Secretary of Navy under President John F. Kennedy, and Secretary of the Treasury under President Richard Nixon. Two of Connally's principal legal clients were Sid Richardson and Perry Bass.)

My father was chosen as a Vigil Honor Member the same evening that I was, in 1967. That was kinda cool. Each Vigil Honor Member goes out into the night alone, and stays awake all night, contemplating beside a campfire, and reflecting on why he is there and on the ideals of the "Brotherhood."

In 1969, I became the Lodge Chief of the Karankawa Lodge of the Order of the Arrow. That's a pretty big deal, because it represents an area covering seventeen South Texas counties. The year after I was Lodge Chief, my brother Bobby held that honor.

Scouting had begun to teach me how to lead when I was just eleven years old. Along with the rank advancements and all things my brothers and I learned in the Boy Scout program through age eighteen, we were fortunate to go to work at the summer camp over on Lake Mathis (now Lake Corpus Christi). Instead of having a typical summer job as many kids did, I spent ten weeks, in each of seven consecutive summers (1965-1972), from age fifteen to twenty-two, working there.

At one time or another, I taught merit badges in the nature area and waterfront area, and I wound up as Aquatics Director. Bobby worked under me on the waterfront staff for a couple of summers, working at the new pool.

We had three hundred boys in camp each week, and maybe fifty to one hundred of them were non-swimmers. They checked in along with the rest of their troop and within a week, Bobby taught most of them how to swim in the pool. He had a pretty good success rate—three out of four, or better.

Since both the Girl Scouts and the Campfire Girls had camps on the lake, as the Boy Scouts did, legend has it we would paddle over to visit them in canoes during our off time.

As staff members, Bobby and I worked around thirty or forty peers who were going through the same camping and leadership experience that we were. We formed lifelong friendships, almost like a fraternity. Now most of us are grandparents, and we still see each other once in a while.

We also had adult leadership mentors that made camp feel like a summer home, and a part of growing up. Some of those individuals became lifetime friends. When one of my mentors, J. Vern Herring, died in 2010, I gave a eulogy at his funeral. I had worked for him for seven summers while he was the director of the camp.

For a few years, when I was just getting started in the adult world, I wasn't too involved in Scouting, but then I took it up again. I had my own son, Collin, and I wanted him to have the same experience I'd had. I put him in Scouting and even became his Scoutmaster eventually.

That was a real challenging period, because it took a lot of my time. I was responsible for a whole troop of boys, and leadership of each of them and the other adults who were working with them too. Planning camp outs and other activities almost consumed my

The day Collin got his Eagle.

life for two and a half years. I enjoyed it, because I got to be around my son at the same time. I'm very proud to say that Collin became an Eagle Scout, just as my brothers and I did.

My sister's two daughters, Kelly Lynn Ahr and Amanda Catherine Ahr, received high honors in Girl Scouts as well. And now Kelly's daughter Carina is involved, and Kelly's two sons, Andrew and Jeremy, became Eagle Scouts. There's another younger son, Braden, who will probably head down the same path as his brothers.

Kids get into Scouting because it's fun. They love to do the outdoor thing—camping and all the stuff that goes with that. But it's a sort of "bait and switch" program, I think.

If I went into a school auditorium, trying to recruit new kids to join Scouting, I could say, "Hey, how many of y'all want to come learn about leadership and character development?" Probably not a one would raise his hand. But when I say, "How many of y'all want to go camping this weekend?" every hand goes up.

Boys come for the fun, and they don't realize that all the time they're enjoying themselves and learning a lot of outdoor skills, they're also learning leadership skills, character development, values and principles.

They learn the Scout Oath. The twelve points of the Scout Law provide a code we all can live by—to be trustworthy, loyal, helpful, friendly, courteous, kind, obedient, cheerful, thrifty, brave, clean, and reverent. It's a basic preparation for all the things we all should do, in terms of duty to God, duty to country, and duty to self. Those are strong principles, applicable to any situation in life.

Boy Scouts learn all this at a young age, and they're having fun doing it. They're not realizing how important this will become to who they are, and who they will be, as individuals.

When Scouting is complemented by good strong family values, church, a good school curriculum, and—for some—athletics, a kid becomes a well rounded person. To me, Scouting is probably the strongest, best youth development program in the world. It has been around for one hundred years, and it's a worldwide organization whose principles and core values have never changed.

In recent years, there has been some unfortunate controversy around the Boy Scout program. That's sad, because Scouting is such an outstanding opportunity for youth development. Truth is, the Boy Scouts have now become co-ed. In our Council, there are even more girls in Boy Scouting than in the Girl Scout program. After a youngster gets to a certain age level, he or she can join this co-ed program called Venture Crew. Even when political pressure and lawsuits attempt to make Scouting bend a little on some of its principles, the program stands firm.

Obviously, parents are the biggest impact on any child's life, and church is right there too, kind of tandem. But for me, Scouting probably rates as the second strongest influence on my life. It has been a huge part of my life, and I give it a lot of credit for developing who I am and always will be as a person. Now I'm helping to provide that experience to others.

I got involved on the Boy Scout Executive Board, which manages the business affairs of the whole South Texas Council—a seventeen county area. I have served in a number of capacities, and in 2010, Camp Karankawa celebrated its sixty-sixth anniversary. That Boy Scout camp, the one I attended for so many years, still had many facilities that hadn't changed in fifty years.

We needed a major renovation, and I became Chairman of the Capital Campaign. Our goal was to bring in $2.4 million, and we reached the $1.4 million mark in the first year, despite the rough economy.

In 1944, only boys and men camped at Karankawa. Today, there are as many moms and siblings involved in camping programs there, as there are Boy Scouts participating in traditional Scout camping activities. Each spring more than 5000 co-ed elementary school children participate in the Learning for Life Character Development program. The facilities are also available to school, church and community groups whose missions and values are compatible with those of Scouting.

Our 130-acre camp on Lake Corpus Christi includes 16 campsites; a large swimming pool; a waterfront with canoes, rowboats, kayaks and sailboats; craft areas; a nature area and trails; an archery range; a rifle and shotgun range; a campfire amphitheater; a trading post; a 300-person dining hall; and a large indoor training center. In addition to the full summer camp operation, the camp is used on weekends all year.

The Rockport-Fulton Chamber of Commerce

New developments popped up all around our area—Key Allegro, in 1962, Cape Velero in the early 1980s, followed by the Rockport Country Club starting in the mid-80s. Some sputtered a little bit, because of what was happening in the oil and gas business. At the same time, some tax incentives related to owning real estate were removed, and that intensified the real estate crunch.

In about 1984-5, the Chamber of Commerce had an annual budget of $50,000, including the office manager's salary and some expenses. The annual advertising budget—which was truly the promotion budget—was just $1500 a year. All the motels, and people who lived here and owned condos and such, did their own marketing.

A group of us in the Rockport-Fulton Area Chamber of Commerce, all in our thirties, wanted to make some changes. We put our stakes down in the middle of all this. We banded together to face the Old Guard—the "but we've always done it this way" people who believed that everything should stay the same.

They called us the "Brat Pack." I was pretty much the leader of that group— the first person, of four chairmen in a row, who wanted to do things differently. We made a lot of changes to the Chamber of Commerce that are still in effect. Though we experienced some tough years, our plan paid off when the economy turned. We were in good position to move forward.

My group of friends in the Chamber believed that it would make sense for everyone in the tourist business to pool their resources. We proposed a three-cent hotel/motel tax, providing funds to promote the community for everyone.

Realizing we faced a real challenge in trying to get the idea approved, I went before the City Council of Rockport, in the old City Hall (now the new site of the Chamber of Commerce), and also at Fulton, We didn't realize how strong that challenge would be! As a young buck in my mid-30s, trying to get this thing done, I got such a reaction from some of the motel owners that you would have thought I was asking for their first-born child!

They worried that adding a three percent tax to the cost of a room would mean that no one would come to their motel. They believed that vacationers who had been coming to Rockport or Fulton would change their plans and go to towns that did not have such a tax.

But gradually some people came to realize the value of our suggestion, and the tax was passed. The $1500 we allotted for promotion in those days has grown remarkably. Our community now has revenues of about $1 million a year to promote tourism! It's no longer a three percent tax; it's seven percent, about the same as everyone else across the state.

Travelers to tourist destinations know that they're likely to have to pay a room tax. No one asks, when checking into a motel, what the tax is. They see it on the bill when they leave, but it's just part of the game. It becomes an afterthought for most people; they don't even consider it. But it was tough, getting it done. I still have holes in my back, but much of what we have enjoyed in this community in the last twenty-five years now can be attributed to the impact resulting from promotion of our tourist industry which we started in the mid-Eighties.

I was elected Chairman of the Rockport-Fulton Area Chamber of Commerce in 1986. Fortunately, that happened to be one of the best years of the decade in the shrimp business. Since I didn't have to spend as much time at the fish house trying to survive, I had more time to devote to my volunteer job. And by that time, the Navigation District lawsuit was behind us, too. Those bits of good fortune freed me to accomplish much more than I might have otherwise.

I contacted Ken Pagans, of the Texas A&M Extension Service. He was really good at long-range planning and had worked on "CC-90" in Corpus Christi—a futuristic thing in the early 1980s, looking forward to 1990. Ken helped me lead a similar program for Rockport-Fulton. We called our long-term strategic planning initiative "Renaissance '86," and some of the people who had worked with Ken in Corpus helped the Rockport-Fulton effort too.

We put together a group of about 125 people in this community, divided into a number of task forces, each made up of about eight members. We looked at various things in the community that needed to be done and put together what amounted to a long-range plan for Rockport.

We totally reorganized the Chamber that year. We started a monthly newsletter, which we'd never had before. We introduced an off-site retreat for the Board. We went to Port Royal, in Port Aransas, and sat around for an overnight-stay weekend, talking about our strategic plan for the year. That had never been done. We formed a Tourism Development Council, a separate committee of the Chamber, to handle all tourism promotion. That still exists today. And on and on . . .

We hired our first Executive Director. We went from an office manager to a hired professional. We interviewed people across the state, to find someone who wanted to come here and run our Chamber the way it should be run. Our first Executive Director was from Oklahoma, but he was here less than two years. Diane Probst came in about 1990. She still holds the job, and the Chamber has earned a Five-Star designation, putting it among the top 1% in the nation.

Many of the things that I started were continued in the next years by other members of the Brat Pack as Chairmen— Michael Meek (1987-88), Susie Bracht Black (1988-89) and Clay Gillis (1989-90).

Meek, Black, and Jackson

The tourism effort became more professional as more local industry experts were involved. Surveys of our members led to new programs. They included: Shoot-the-Hoop basketball tourney fundraiser for the band; Bay Bucks program; Operation Spotlight award. We adopted a two-mile stretch of highway to keep clean; we met with the City regarding the beach park logo and painting the band shell. We helped accelerate the Maritime Museum's construction, through grants from Perry Bass and the Sid Richardson Foundation.

The HummerBird Celebration developed on Susie Bracht Black's watch—in September of 1988. Mike Meek went on to become a professional in the business and is still the CEO of the New Braunfels, Texas, Chamber of Commerce. Unfortunately, Clay Gillis was killed in a plane crash some years later, but he definitely left his mark as well.

The Rockport Beach Park wasn't a Chamber of Commerce initiative, but we were involved in getting it done, with the support of Rockport Mayor Burt Mills and the City Council. And countless other things over the years.

The Chamber of Commerce was basically a turn-around story. When I look back on my life, most of the things I've been involved in were turn-arounds of some kind or another. That's just something I've always wanted to do—not to just do something small, but to make a large and lasting positive difference. Plenty of people are willing to do small things, but I'm one of the ones who want to do whatever it takes to make a permanent and significant improvement in a situation or an organization.

The Education Foundation

Another significant challenge came along in 1999, when the high school principal, Wayne Johnson (who later became Superintendent), put me on a site-based committee. Our task was to figure out a way to get the community involved in the schools. My daughter Sarah had just graduated from high school and my son Collin was still there, so I had my antennae up, trying to figure out what we could do.

Coincidentally, in December, 2000, I went to an investment industry conference, part of a panel of four to speak there. The conference, at the Hyatt Regency Hotel in Beaver Creek, Colorado, lasted several days, providing me an opportunity to visit some of the other presentations.

One of them was the concept of an Education Foundation. Teachers probably do the most important job in the world, but most of the time, in our society, they don't get reasonable pay. They don't get much recognition, either. The Education Foundation provides that recognition. With an annual fund drive, and special events, the Foundation raises money in the community, mostly from private sector people, and pools those funds.

A Grants Committee receives applications from the teachers in the district and invites them to present innovative teaching projects for consideration. These should be projects that could never get funded through the normal School Board budget, something way beyond that. Then the Foundation comes up with a way to fund it.

As I listened to the conference speaker, I thought, "I'll bet we could do that in Rockport."

Then I thought again: Since I had never heard of such a thing, maybe it was not legal in Texas. As soon as I got home, I went to the school superintendent, Adrian Johnson, to ask about that. "Oh, yeah," he told me. "We had one of those in Corsicana."

But I still didn't know enough about it. Eventually, I learned that Dr. Pete Karabatsos, from Colorado, puts those things together for schools. When I contacted him, he said, "Sure, we can help you do that."

I recruited ten people to help me get The Education Foundation going. I got some seed money to pay Karabatsos. He and his team came down here from their base in Colorado, and he walked us through setting up a 501C-3, and all of the by-laws and committees, and how it should be structured, and how to raise money, and so on.

For eight months in 2001, we met monthly, and in August we held our first organizational corporate board meeting. We scheduled our first official board meeting for September 11, 2001.

What timing! In the middle of one of the bleakest periods of our country's history, we were starting an Education Foundation. Of course we postponed that first Board meeting.

When we finally got started, we had a 27-member board in the beginning, a working board that met every month. On top of that, we had the Grant Committee, and about eight other committees.

In the first few years, ten or twenty teachers put together grant proposals. Using very strict criteria, we chose about half of them to fund. In the first six or eight years, we gave away, each year, about $60,000 *in cash*, to school teachers. And that was a very big deal.

The teachers could use the cash to buy a program or equipment or something that was really 'outside the box,' something that put their students a notch ahead. We gave them an opportunity to do something that they would never have been able to do in Rockport, Texas. And now, as a result, when our kids go to college, they can compete favorably with kids in Houston and Dallas, and all the big cities. The kids are the beneficiaries, because they have a larger tool kit than they ever had before.

It's a great concept, and there was a lot of publicity with this program, so people started joining us. The community caught on to it, and the organization is really flying now.

In ten years, we took The Education Foundation from the germ of an idea to an extraordinary organization in this community. It has become the 'charity of choice' here, for people who really believe in helping young people achieve their potential.

Since 2001, we have brought the Corpus Christi Symphony Orchestra to the Rockport-Fulton High School auditorium once a year. This is an outstanding symphony, world class.

We now pay them for a Christmas-time Sunday afternoon concert to a packed house. Our high school choir is on stage with the symphony orchestra. The music is great; it's a 'feel good' thing. It's not so much a money-maker as a way for the kids to rub elbows with professionals on the same stage.

After the concert, everyone goes over to the high school Commons area, where we stage Flavor of Success. Fifteen to twenty local restaurants present free refreshments, while throughout the room, teachers and kids show off how they used their grant money. It's an opportunity for everyone to see what The Education Foundation does.

In late April, we present Shining Stars Over Aransas, a program that recognizes graduating seniors and fits in with the overall mission of the foundation. Let's say there are 200 graduating seniors, so about twenty of them are among the top ten percent, according to their high school grade point averages. We recognize them, but also recognize twenty or so more kids who may be good at just one thing.

They may be C students, but they are excellent in a single area. The teachers in each department—an academic department, not athletics—get together and pick out an outstanding student or two in their field. Those students, many of whom have never been recognized in their lives, are on the same stage with those "straight A" students.

We have a nice sit-down dinner on white tablecloths, in the Commons area, and put these 40-45 students on a pedestal. It's a very moving ceremony—music, video, you name it. The parents are out there, and the families, and the teachers. And here's the kicker: Each one of those students gets to invite an educator who made a difference in his or her life. It could be a third-grade teacher, or one from junior high, or high school. The student could even choose to honor an educator now deceased. When each of those students goes up to the podium, the teacher that he or she is recognizing goes up there too. Talk about emotional!

I've had teachers tell me, after that event, that it was about the most important moment in their careers—more than any money, or anything they ever got: public recognition, by one of the students they taught—maybe ten or twelve years earlier. I'm very proud of that organization.

In 2007, we established a million dollar endowment as a part of this program. That was a real challenge. We don't have a million dollars in cash, but we do have a million in commitments. We got cash from some people, long-term pledges from others, life-insurance policies, real estate—creating a funding source in perpetuity. Nobody else in our area has done that. Other organizations have endowment-type funds, but we're the only one with a million dollar endowment.

When the high school principal, Wayne Johnson, first asked a committee of us to figure out a way to get the community involved in the schools, I had no idea how much the general public could get caught up in it.

Today, of our thirty-plus member board, only about five have kids in school— or ever had kids in school here. Most are retirees who didn't even live here themselves while growing up. But they have a commitment to education.

What I noticed, when I started recruiting for that board, and for the whole project, is that a common thread among us all is that we can relate to some teacher who helped turn us around, or influenced our thinking, or helped us set our future direction. Some of us may go to one particular church or another; we may like art, or museums, or history. But we all relate to education; it's a common thread among us.

That's why it wasn't so hard to make this project work. I thought it was going to be a tough job, but it wasn't at all difficult to get people excited about The Education Foundation.

I finally rotated off as president in 2009, and a retired attorney is running the Foundation now. He's very sincere, and is doing a great job. The Education Foundation has meant a great deal to me. It's an example of starting something from ground zero, and something that I have a lot of pride in. And it all began while I was attending a conference about investments. But then, you know, education really is the best investment of all.

Corpus Christi Symphony Orchestra

Bringing the Symphony to Rockport on behalf of The Education Foundation in 2001 resulted in my placement on the symphony's board. I served for eight years, and rolled off in 2009. During the time I was on the board, we learned that John Giordano, internationally-known conductor of the Fort Worth Symphony, was transitioning into retirement. He had a love for the coast and for sailing, so when we had an opening, we approached him. Much to our amazement, he accepted our offer and has now been with the Corpus Christi Symphony Orchestra for several years.

The combination of a world-class conductor, quality musicians, and a superb Performing Arts Center at Texas A&M Corpus Christi has really taken the orchestra to a new level. Like most such orchestras, the Corpus Christi Symphony has struggled financially, but it is clearly one of the best-kept secrets in South Texas.

Aransas County Historical Society

We'd had an Aransas County Historical Commission for some time. In 1985, we formed The Aransas County Historical Society, primarily to provide a tax deduction for those who wanted to contribute to saving and moving the Stella Maris Chapel in Lamar. I was the organizing president, as I recall—just on paper. Other people took it and ran with it, developing a mission to "identify, protect, record, and interpret historic and prehistoric sites, structures, papers, records, and artifacts relating to the unique environment and evolution of the county, to share all with the public, and to promote the appreciation of history within the area."

This organization has really prospered in recent years and has generated lots of interest in local history.

Rockport Center for the Arts

Beginning with my great-grandmother, Irene Barton Norvell, our family has always had an art connection, both in performing and visual arts, so it seemed only natural for me to be involved as well. I served on the Board of the Rockport Center of the Arts in 1995 and 1996, then became President in 1997. During that time, we conceived the idea of writing a county history, and I was on the steering committee that made it a reality. The final result was *ARANSAS: The Life of a Texas Coastal County*, by William Allen and Sue Hastings. It is accepted as the definitive history of our area and is required reading for every new member of Leadership Aransas County.

That leadership program, sponsored by the Rockport-Fulton Chamber of Commerce, is under the direction of Chamber Executive Director Diane Probst. Those who are selected for enrollment in the program commit to nine months of intense work and become great, informed leaders for our area. I actually played a role in the original founding of the leadership class.

When I was president of the Art Association board in 1997, we brought the international group "Up With People" to Rockport, and they came twice more after that. "Up With People" formed in the Sixties and had up to 500 young adults in each of five casts who traveled the world in a cultural exchange format. They would spend several days in a host city and lived with host families. Although they did a lot of community service and cultural exchange, they also performed a Broadway-quality musical production in each of the cities they visited.

Our family was so impressed with the program that our daughter Sarah took off from college one year to tour with them. Unfortunately, half way through that year, while Sarah's cast was in Europe, financial issues forced the organization to cease operations.

In 1998, my sister Mary Lucille became Executive Director of the Rockport Center for the Arts, a position she held until her retirement in October, 2005.

So the arts have been a very important part of our family's heritage in Rockport for 125 years. ❧

TAKING THE TIDE

PART VI
SUCH A FULL SEA

Today

Once I got out of school, I hardly even watched sports, much less played. The shrimp business provided me with plenty of physical activity, so I didn't need too much exercise. When I got in the investment business, I didn't have much opportunity to work out. But then I turned fifty and resolved to run in the Beach to Bay Marathon in Corpus Christi. It's a six-person relay marathon, with each person running 4.4 miles, and I ran one of the legs on a Rockport team in May of 2000.

I started to train for it in January, getting up before daylight. At first, I ran just a couple of miles, and worked my way up to three or four miles to get in shape.

The race began out on Padre Island, at Bob Hall Pier. My 4.4 mile leg began near the Naval Air Station. I ran along the bayshore, and then onto Ocean Drive. By about 10:30 on that morning in late May, I noticed how much the weather had warmed up, compared to my "early-morning run" schedule in previous months. Competing with hundreds of people got my adrenaline flowing, so I ran faster than I had trained. And I was breathing in car fumes from the traffic on Ocean Drive.

With the combination of those three things—heat, adrenaline, and auto exhaust—I barely completed my leg of the race. When I came across my 4.4 mile mark at one of the pocket parks on Ocean Drive, I fell to my knees.

Debbie was there. One of the race officials, a paramedic, took my temperature, and it was 105°! They were so scared that they took me to Spohn Hospital by ambulance. I had an IV to rehydrate my body, and I lay there, trying to remember whether or not I had given my baton to the next racer. I was going crazy with worry about it. Even later that night, at a party, all I could talk about was, "Did I hand off that baton?"

After that experience, Debbie said, "No more." But since I had started running again just as I turned fifty, I determined that I wouldn't stop, and I never have. I don't run marathons, but I still jog in the morning, three or four days a week.

I don't like jogging at the end of the day; I want to do it in the morning, when

I'm fresh. I have a little route through the neighborhood. From my house to the cemetery and back is about 1.6 miles—not very far, but enough to keep me in shape. I don't run real fast, so it takes me 16-17 minutes. I break a sweat and get a little out of breath; I know I've had a workout.

I feel really good in the morning, after I've done that. It gives me some cardio and helps me maintain my weight. I eat like a horse, but jogging keeps me from gaining too much weight. If I really wanted to lose weight, I could probably eat less and keep jogging to do that. I wish I did some weight training, too. I'd like to do a lot of physical things, but I don't do as much anymore, except at the ranch on weekends.

One of my little-known passions is music—almost any kind of music. Through-out my entire life, at whatever stage, music has always played a significant part of my personal enjoyment. This appreciation for music, and my ability to read music, is probably one of the mostly-inherited traits I received from my mother, and I love her for that. Probably some genes from my father's side of the family helped too, since Nana (Great-grandmother Irene Norvell) was also a musician.

In my opinion, the music of the '60s and '70s, when I was growing up, has never been matched. That period in our nation's history spawned some of the greatest talents in songwriting and musical expression. Even my kids enjoy it to this day. I've also taken a liking to country and western music through the years, and Debbie and I love to dance.

I consider the era of the Great Depression an example of hope in the midst of adversity. The people who worked their way through that are the greatest genera-tion, I believe. Younger people, who have not been through tough times, don't know—can't appreciate—overcoming obstacles to get where they want to be. I think that someone who has lived through tough times can be a better person because of it.

Adversity builds character. When we come back from the abyss, we prove that we can practice what we preach.

We overcome obstacles.

We refuse to give up.

We persevere.

Tomorrow

So we arrive at this day, and try to see the next one coming. For a century and a quarter, my family has loved the magnificent swath of beach and bay that defines Rockport. We have dreamed over it, struggled with it, overcome defeat and heartbreak, laughed and played and rejoiced in the rich beauty and bounty of this special God-blessed place.

Literally hundreds of people, and dozens of families, have worked and lived and played along this piece of waterfront. But of all the owners and tenants of this acreage through the years, the Jacksons, on the north end, had the longest uninterrupted chain of title.

When we sold our property in 1990, we conveyed to Rockport Harborfront, L.P., 3200 lineal feet of waterfront, all bulkheaded, with sixteen-plus acres behind the bulkhead, right in the center of town.

The property lies within the Rockport Heritage District, and almost everything that ever happened of importance in the City and County happened within this six-block area, beginning with the arrival of Zachary Taylor on our Rocky Point.

In my office, I have a file drawer filled with dreams—all those plats, drawings, and surveys that were a part of our law suit over the land. Old dreams of developing the rocky point, and dreams of what could be if the point were blasted away.

In 1848, a newcomer to the area envisioned a great western port at Lamar, connected by rail lines to Goliad and San Antonio. Nothing much came of it. In 1910, a land-promotion group planned to turn Rockport into a great city. Ocean liners would bring tourists to our shore. This visionary believed that the U.S. government should establish a great naval base and dry docks here, linking the military bases at San Antonio to the new Panama Canal. A railroad running from Rockport to Harbor Island would eliminate commercial clutter in our city.

After the 1919 hurricane, the U.S. Congress decided to provide funds for a deepwater harbor somewhere in the vicinity of the Aransas pass. Rockport and the town of Aransas Pass rivaled Corpus Christi for those funds. But Corpus got the nod, and the port.

In 1971, Aransas County Judge John Wendell commented on a new move to deepen water from Port Aransas to Aransas Pass and the Conn Brown harbor. He believed it was a "must" that the Aransas County Navigation District deepen our channel too, so that ships could come to Rockport. He believed we might develop a large port for foreign shipping. But Rockport remained small.

My file holds more recent drawings too—the dreams of modern developers who catch the spirit of this place, the potential of what this piece of land can be. Dreams of art colonies, nature sanctuaries, and luxury homes.

All these dreams arise, I believe, because this piece of land marks the heart of the Coastal Bend and holds the essence of Texas. Here we have known, and still find, families and loners, cowboys and seafarers, carpetbaggers and oil men. The wealthiest of the wealthy, and the most modest of weekend vacationers.

From Market Street to the Fish Bowl harbor, Austin Street borders the waterfront property. It lures locals and visitors to shops, art galleries, museums, an aquarium, a beach park and the Chamber of Commerce. But on the shoreline east of Austin Street—incredible as it seems—the land lies barren.

Over the years since we ceded our property there, City fathers developed a long-range master plan very similar to the one I had envisioned, now more than a quarter-century ago.

There have been a few false starts and a couple of recessions along the way, but I am convinced that someday, when the current serves, someone will carefully develop and preserve this acreage. Here is one developer's vision, among several that have been considered.

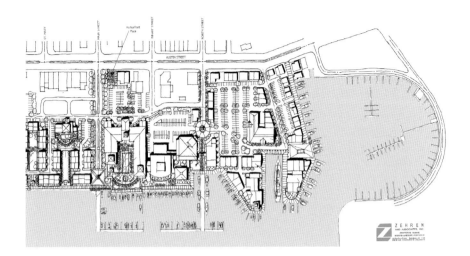

There will be more dreams, I am sure—probably more varied than I can begin to imagine. But I believe that as Rockport's waterfront becomes vital once more, it will develop in its own distinctive way.

I believe that old-fashioned values of family and integrity will guide us. We have learned that less can be more, and that quality matters more than quantity. We can all live the dream, in the turning of the tides at this very special place. ❧

TAKING THE TIDE

APPENDIX

TIMELINE

1165	William de Bolling, Jackson ancestor, owns land in England
1519	Spaniards explore Rockport area
1620-30	Hugh Norvell lays out town of Williamsburg, Virginia
1683	Norvell family builds home in Virginia
1684	LaSalle maps Rockport area shoreline
1715	Benjamin Jackson born in Ireland
1737	Isaac Jackson born in Pennsylvania
1738	Thomas Barton born
1746	Spaniards built Fort Aranzasu on Live Oak Point
1799	Richard Walker Barton born in Virginia
1805	Stephen Jackson born in Georgia
1817	Pirate Jean Lafitte on San Jose Island
	James Power & James Hewetson apply for colonial grant at Aransas Bay
1834	Power's colonists sail into Aransas Bay
1835	Enoch Milton Jackson born in Alabama
1836	Texas declares independence from Mexico
1841-43	Barton serves in U.S. House with Daniel Webster
1845	Texas joins Union; Zachary Taylor lands at the Rocky Point
1857	Elisha Hundley Norvell born in Virginia
1861	Texas secedes from the Union
1865	Irene Barton born in Virginia
1867	Doughty & Mathis build wharf on Rocky Point, found town of Rockport
1883-4	Irene Barton teaching at Centenary Institute, Alabama
1885	Elisha Norvell marries Irene Barton in Alabama
1886	Elisha and Irene Norvell hired to teach at Goliad College, Texas
1888	SAAP Railroad reaches Rockport
Aug 1888	Elisha and Irene Norvell move to Rockport, bringing with them her parents, Rev. and Mrs. R.T. Barton
1889	Irene Barton Norvell born

1906	Jacksons buy waterfront property
1913	Irene Barton Norvell marries S. F. Jackson
1914	Norvells build house at 801 N. Magnolia as wedding present to Irene
1915	Norvell Ford Jackson born at 801 N. Magnolia
1919	Neva Miles Porter born
	S.F. Jackson buys brother's interest in seafood business
	Devastating hurricane hits Rockport
1925	State Highway 35 & Intracoastal Waterway system begin
	Aransas County Navigation District formed
1930	SAAP rail no longer in use
	S.F. Jackson purchases railroad pier
1935	Jackson Channel and Dock Company formed
1936	Aransas County Navigation District receives State patent for submerged lands
1938	Norvell Jackson graduates from University of Texas, forms Jackson Sales Co.
1940	Neva Porter and Norvell Jackson marry
1941	U.S. enters World War II
1942	Norvell Jackson enlists in Army Air Force
	Mary Lucille Jackson born
1945	Norvell Jackson discharged from military
1946	Norvell Ford Jackson, Jr., born
1950	John Porter Jackson born
1951	Robert Milton Jackson born
1958	Jacksons build ice plant
1960s	RYSCO building boats
1961	Hurricane Carla
1962	Jackson Shipyard burns
1963	Morrison Boathouses burn
1966	Jackson Boathouses burn again

1967	Hurricane Beulah
1970	S.F. Jackson dies
	James B. Jackson dies
	Hurricane Celia
1971	Jackson adds steel boats to its fleet
1974	John P. Jackson receives MBA at Texas A&I; joins family business
1976	John Jackson and Debbie Carlisle marry
	Exclusive Economic Zone established in Gulf of Mexico
1978	Jackson installs automatic ice rake, hardware store, new fuel tanks
1979	Jackson sets up scallop boat operation, Newport News, Virginia
1980	Scallop boats return to Texas from Florida
1981	Jacksons take fleet to Colombia
	Sarah Jackson born
1982	Jacksons begin company Reorganization
1983	Jackson sues Aransas County Navigation District to clear land title
1985	Collin Jackson born
	Oil and gas business and real estate downturn
1985-87	Jackson tries bottom long-lining in Texas and calico scalloping in Florida
1986-87	John Jackson leads Rockport-Fulton Area Chamber of Commerce as Chairman
1990	Jackson sells waterfront property to Bass family
1991	Jackson sells fleet of boats
1992	John Jackson joins nationwide investment firm
1995	John Jackson opens investment offices in Rockport, at Live Oak Plaza
1997	Neva Jackson passes away
2002	Norvell Jackson passes away
2008	John Jackson moves investment practice from Live Oak Plaza to 2902 Traylor Boulevard

FAMILY TREES

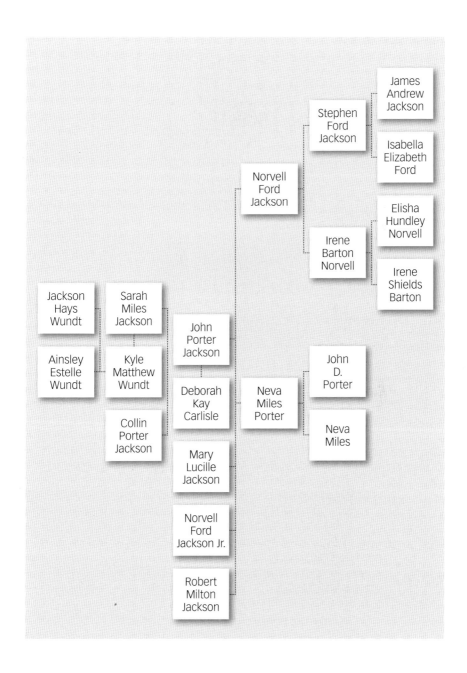

FAMILY TREES

DESCENDANTS OF JAMES ANDREW JACKSON

1 James Andrew Jackson, b. 8/10/1856 in Coosa County AL; d 1/12/1914 in Pasadena, TX
  + Isabella Elizabeth Ford, b 9/3/1858 in DeSoto Parish LA; m 1880; d 8/19/ 1894 in Hollis, Madison County, TX
    2 Roy Jackson, b 11/24/1880; d 12/19/1967
      + Geraldine O'Neil, m 1905
    2 Benjamin Dee Jackson; b 11/6/1882; d 4/24/1924
      + Lillie Tisdale, m abt 1908
    2 Annie Jackson, b 5/25/1884; d 3/13/1976
      + James Edward Brook, m Jan 1903
    2 Joshua Milton Jackson, b 7/14/1892; d 4/28/1952
      + Fern Zelma McCook, m abt 1920
        3 Joshua Milton Jackson, Jr., b 12/24/1927
          + Johnelle deBrueys, b 8/17/1927; m 6/9/1948
    2 Isabella Jackson, b 1894; d 1980
    2 Stephen Ford Jackson, b 8/25/1886 in Hollis, Madison County, TX, d 2/16/1970 in Corpus Christi TX
      + Irene Barton Norvell, b 3/14/1891 in Rockbridge or Bedford Co., VA; m 6/25/1913 in Rockport, TX; d 2/8/1973 in Corpus Christi TX
        3 Norvell Ford Jackson b 6/29/15 in Rockport, TX, d 2/1/2002 in Rockport, TX
          + Neva Miles Porter, b 11/18/1919 in Mineral Wells, TX, m 10/30/1940, d 5/29/1997 in Corpus Christi, TX
            4 Mary Lucille Jackson, b 10/30/1942 in Corpus Christi, TX
              + Wayne Merrill Ahr, b 12/11/1938 in San Antonio, TX, m 1961 (div.)
                5 Kelly Lynn Ahr, b 8/11/1962 in Bryan, TX
                  + Louis Scott Biar, b 11/15/1963 in Beaumont, TX
                    6 Andrew Jackson Biar, b 5/28/1992 in Houston, TX
                    6 Jeremy Wayne Biar, b 8/24/1994 in Houston, TX
                    6 Carina Grace Biar, b 2/28/2001 in Houston, TX
                    6 Braden Carl Biar, b 3/8/2003 in Houston, TX
                5 Amanda Catherine Ahr, b 12/7/1968 in Houston, TX
                  + Matthew Graham Snyder, b 8/23/1972 in Beirut, Lebanon, (div.)
                    6 Oliver Graham Snyder, b 1/21/07in Houston, TX
            4 Norvell Ford Jackson, Jr., b 6/8/1946 in Corpus Christi, TX
            4 John Porter Jackson, b 10/21/1950 in Corpus Christi, TX
              + Deborah Kay Carlisle, b 9/4/1951 in Alice, TX; m 7/23/1976
                5 Sarah Miles Jackson, b 5/6/1981 in Kingsville, TX
                  + Kyle Matthew Wundt, b 10/19/1976 in Seguin, TX
                    6 Jackson Hays Wundt, b 7/20/2008 in New Braunfels, TX

6 Ainsley Estelle Wundt, b 12/1/2009 in New Braunfels, TX
5 Collin Porter Jackson, b 4/4/1985 in Corpus Christi, TX
4 Robert Milton Jackson, b 12/5/1951, in Austin, TX
3 James Barton Jackson, b 3/12/1917 in Rockport TX; d 2/28/1970, in Houston, TX
+ Mary Elizabeth Gilbert, b 12/25/1918; d 10 /25/1991 in Houston, TX
    4 James Gilbert Jackson, b 7/5/1944
      + Patricia Gregg, b 4/21/1946
    4 Annie Irene (Nan) Jackson, b 12/26/1945
    4 Frederick Barton Jackson, b 1/24/1951
      + Deborah Kay Boller, b 8/2/1952
    4 Mary "Molly" Ulrich Jackson, b 11/19/1955
      + John Owen, b 10/8/1956
3 Isabel Irene Jackson, b 1/21/1919, in Rockport, TX, d 9/6/1996 in New Braunfels, TX
+ Evans Foster Corbin, b 3/11/1916 in Carlinville, IL, d 12/11/1994 in New Braunfels, TX
    4 James Evans Corbin, b 10/4/41 in Greenville, MS, d 11/26/2004 in Nacogdoches, TX
    4 Edward Ford Corbin, b 4/5/1943 in Rockport, TX
      + Niki Louise Dick, b 2/2/1946 in Ft. Worth, TX
    4 Anna Irene Corbin, b 2/2/1946 in Corpus Christi, TX
      + Carl Glenn Williams, b 10/30/1942 in Houston, TX
    4 John Paul Corbin, b 7/16/1948 in Corpus Christi, TX
      + Cynthia Terese Williams, b 9/3/1964 in Jackson, MS
3 Annie Ruth Jackson, b 9/21/1924; d 8/19/2000 in Taft, TX
+ Maynard Abrahams, b 10/22/19, d 10/4/2009 in Wayne, KS
    4 Stephen Merle Abrahams, b 11/28/1948 in San Antonio, TX
      + Mona Ann Daum, b 8/23/1954 in Lewiston, MT
    4 Karen Ruth Abrahams, b 11/29/1952 in San Antonio, TX
      + Cliff Turner, b 8/15/50 in Newton, IA
3 Mary Virginia Jackson, b 11/18/1926 in Taft TX, d 5/15/2008 in Houston, TX
+ Bruce Gordon Davis, b 9/02/1922 in Fulton TX; m 8/31/1946 in Corpus Christi, TX
    4 Ford Rouquette Davis, b 12/19/1948 in Austin, TX
      + Mary Ann Miller, b 10/15/1950 in Wichita Falls, TX
    4 Barton Bolling Davis, b 2/5/1952 in Corpus Christi, TX
      + Ann Angela Kostas, b 3/18/1953 in Baytown, TX
    4 Katherine Norvell Davis, b 2/25/1954 in Ft. Sam Houston, TX
      + Paul Campbell McLendon, b 11/11/1952 in TX

FAMILY TREES

DESCENDANTS OF RICHARD WALKER BARTON

1 Richard Walker Barton, b 3/7/1799 in "Springdale," Winchester, Frederick Co, VA;
d 1/15/1860 in Bartonsville, Frederick Co, VA

+ Alcinda Winn Gibson, b 4/2/1800 in VA; m 11/14/1822 in VA; d 12/12/1892 in Culpeper Co, VA

    2 Richard Thomas Barton (Rev.), b 3/31/1826 in "Springdale," Winchester, Frederick Co, VA;
    d 101/2/1889 in Corpus Christi, TX

    + Sarah Jane Moore, b 12/29/1830 in Rockbridge Co VA; m 1857; 12/30/1901 in Marion, Smyth Co, VA

        3 Irene Shields Barton, b 5/18/1865 in Rockbridge or Bedford Co, VA;
        d 1/1/1944 in Corpus Christi, TX

        + Elisha Hundley Norvell, b 1/29/1857 in Charlotte C.H., VA; m 1/21/1885 in Summerfield,
        Dallas Co AL; d 11/18/1933 in Corpus Christi, TX

            4 Irene Barton Norvell, b 3/14/1891 in Rockbridge or Bedford Co, VA; d 2/8/1973
            in Corpus Christi, TX

            + Stephen Ford Jackson, b 8/25/1886 in Hollis, Madison Co TX; m 6/25/1913 in Rockport,
            TX; d 2/16 1970 in Corpus Christi TX

                5 Norvell Ford Jackson, b 6/29/1915 in Rockport, TX; d 2/1/2002 in Rockport,TX

                + Neva Miles Porter, b 11/18/1919 in Mineral Wells, TX; m 10/30/1940; d 5/29/1997
                in Corpus Christi, TX

                6 Mary Lucille Jackson, b 10/30/1942 in Corpus Christi, TX

                + Wayne Merrill Ahr, b 12/11/1938 in San Antonio, TX, m 1961 (div.)

                7 Kelly Lynn Ahr, b 8/11/1962 in Bryan, TX

                + Louis Scott Biar, b 11/15/1963 in Beaumont, TX

                8 Andrew Jackson Biar, b 5/28/1992 in Houston, TX

                8 Jeremy Wayne Biar, b 8/24/1994 in Houston, TX

                8 Carina Grace Biar, 2/28/2001 in Houston, TX

                8 Braden Biar, b 3/8/2003 in Houston, TX

                7 Amanda Catherine Ahr, b 12/7/1968 in Houston, TX

                + Matthew Graham Snyder, b 8/23/1972 in Beirut,Lebanon, (div.)

                8 Oliver Graham Snyder, b 1/21/07in Houston, TX

              6 Norvell Ford Jackson, Jr., b 6/8/1946 in Corpus Christi, TX

              6 John Porter Jackson, b 10/21/1950 in Corpus Christi, TX

              + Deborah Kay Carlisle, b 9/4/1951 in Alice, TX; m 7/23/1976

                7 Sarah Miles Jackson, b 5/6/1981 in Kingsville, TX

                + Kyle Matthew Wundt, b 10/19/1976 in Seguin, TX

                8 Jackson Hays Wundt, b 7/20/2008 in New Braunfels, TX

                8 Ainsley Estelle Wundt, b 12/1/2009 in New Braunfels, TX

              7 Collin Porter Jackson, b 4/4/1985 in Corpus Christi, TX

6 Robert Milton Jackson, b 12/5/1951, in Austin, TX
5 James Barton Jackson, b 3/12/1917 in Rockport TX; d 2/28/1970, in Houston, TX
  + Mary Elizabeth Gilbert, b 12/25/1918; d 10/25/1991 in Houston, TX
    6 James Gilbert Jackson, b 7/5/1944
      + Patricia Gregg, b 4/21/1946
    6 Annie Irene (Nan) Jackson, b 12/26/1945
    6 Frederick Barton Jackson, b 1/24/1951
      + Deborah Kay Boller, b 8/2/1952
    6 Mary "Molly" Ulrich Jackson, b 11/19/1955
      + John Owen, b 10/8/1956
5 Isabel Irene Jackson, b 1/21/1919, in Corpus Christi, TX; d 9/6/1996 in New Braunfels, TX
  + Evans Foster Corbin, b 3/11/1916 in Carlinville IL, d 12/11/1994, in New Braunfels, TX
    6 James Evans Corbin, b 10/4/1941 in Greenville, MS, d 11/26/2004 in Nacogdoches, TX
    6 Edward Ford Corbin, b 4/5/1943 in Rockport, TX
      + Niki Louise Dick, b 2/2/1946 in Fort Worth, TX
    6 Anna Irene Corbin, b 2/2/1946 in Corpus Christi, TX
      + Carl Glenn Williams, b 10/30/1942 in Houston, TX
    6 John Paul Corbin, b 7/16/1948 in Corpus Christi, TX
      + Cynthia Terese Williams, b 9/3/1964 in Jackson, MS
5 Annie Ruth Jackson, b 9/21/1924; d 8/19/2000 in Taft, TX
  + Maynard Lyn Abrahams, b 10/22/1919; d 10/4/2009 in Wayne, KS
    6 Stephen Merle Abrahams, b 11/28/1948 in San Antonio, TX
      + Mona Ann Daum, b 8/23/1954 in Lewiston, MT
    6 Karen Ruth Abrahams, b 11/29/1952 in San Antonio, TX
      + Cliff Turner, b 8/15/1950 in Newton, IA
5 MaryVirginia Jackson, b 11/18/1926 in Taft, TX; d 5/15/2008 in Houston, TX
  + Bruce Gordon Davis, b 9/02/1922 in Fulton, TX; m 8/31/1946 in Corpus Christi, TX
    6 Ford Rouquette Davis, b 12/29/1948 in Austin, TX
      + Mary Ann Miller, b 10/15/1950 in Wichita Falls
    6 Barton Bolling Davis, b 2/5/1952 in Corpus Christi, TX
      + Ann Angela Kostas, b 3/18/1953 in Baytown, TX
    6 Katherine Norvell Davis, b 2/25/1954 in Ft. Sam Houston,TX
      + Paul Campbell McLendon, b 11/11/1952 in Beaumont, TX

FAMILY ALBUM

The whole family

Texaco business

1954

The 1940 photograph that Bill Bauer gave me.

"The Old Guys" pose at Mills Wharf.
Daddy is 2nd from left

Daddy and
Grandmother

Quonset hut

1948. Courtesy of Aransas County Historical Society

Church Centennial

Daddy with Mary Lucille's daughters
Amanda (L) and Kelly Ahr

Daddy's 80th Birthday

Debbie's parents,
Gerald and Sue Carlisle

1998

Christening the *Deb-San J*

At Bobby's wedding, late 1980s
NF, Bobby, Mary Lucille, and me

Collin's
high school
graduation party

2006

July 2001
In Hawaii to renew our
wedding vows, with Cathy
Rehmet and my brother
Bobby. They were our maid of
honor and best man on our
wedding day and stood up
with us again on this happy
occasion.

Just Collin

A hunting trip turned into a fishing bonanza

Yankee Stadium with Debbie and Cathy Rehmet

Senior Ring,
High School
Graduation

2003 Graduation

Just Sarah

The fuzziest one is Tigger

Sarah's Senior Photo, 1999

Sarah and Kyle's wedding rehearsal and reception

Kyle's parents,
Ellen and Jim Wundt

Family vacations

The rope leads from
my waist to Sarah's
at Purgatory
Ski Resort, Colorado

Disney World

Natural Bridge Cavern

Ambergris Caye

Cozumel

Catamaran boat trip 2000

Montana

Renewing wedding vows, July 2001

The Grandchildren

Jackson   Ainsley

At the ranch, October 2010

JACKSON Seafood CO. INC.

SUPPLY & SERVICE
DIVISION

SEAFOOD PRODUCTION
DIVISION

P.O. Box 1088
ROCKPORT, TEXAS 78382
Phone: 729-2201

FEATURING:
Complete Trawler Supplies
Fuel & Ice Dock
Net Shop
Trawler Unloading Docks
Welding & Fabrication Shop

Fresh Shrimp
Fresh Deep Water Fin Fish

September 4, 1985

Named for "Yaya,"
my Grandfather,
Stephen Ford Jackson

Named for my Great-Grandmother

Long dock before we had warehouse—ca. 1976

Main Building, Rockport Harbor

One of our wood hulls.

Old net shop, door shop, and warehouse, 1960s

Austin Street & RYSCO

Scallop Dredge

Dipped shrimp nets drying;
fuel tank in background

Long-lining rig

TAKING THE TIDE

Cartagena

"Why is there never time to do a job well,
but always time to do it over?"

"Riverview," the Norvell home in Virginia

Documents

CERTIFICATE OF MEMBERSHIP

This certifies that

Norvell Ford Jackson

has been duly initiated a member of

THE DELTA THETA PHI LAW FRATERNITY

and is entitled to all the rights and privileges of membership therein Initiated by *Sam Houston* Senate. Given under our hands and the seal of this Fraternity this 17th day of May 1937.

Chancellor

Vice Chancellor

No. 15788. *Master of Rolls*

JACKSON BROS. CO.

SHIPPERS OF

FISH : OYSTERS

PRESENTED BY S. F. JACKSON   ROCKPORT, TEXAS

C 212

No. ......

Release of Vendor's Lien

Compared

A. R. Larimer

TO

Roy Jackson

. FILED FOR RECORD

This 25th day of *November* A.D. 190 8
at 3 40 o'clock P. M.

John C. Herring

County Clerk

By ....
Deputy

RECORDED

.... A. D. 190 ....

In .... County Record

of .... Book ....

Page ....

County Clerk

By : ....
Deputy

Recording Fee $ 75 ¢ *paid*

This release should be filed with the County
Clerk immediately for record.

MARTIN, DALLAS

The State of Texas

County of _Aransas_

WHEREAS _D. R. Scrivner and wife, Lula Scrivner_ of the County of _Aransas_ State of _Texas_ did, on the _1st_ day of _August_ A.D. 190 _7_ by deed of that date, duly recorded in the Records of Deeds _Aransas_ County, volume _V_ page _296-7_ Grant, Sell and Convey to _Roy Jackson_ of the County of _Aransas_ State of _Texas_ the following described property, to-wit:

all that tract or parcel of land lying and being situate in the Smith and Wood division of the City of Rockport, Aransas county, Texas, and described as follows, to-wit: Beginning at a point on the South boundary line of Block A, 143 feet from the S. W. corner of said block; Thence North 100 feet; Thence East on a line parallel with the South boundary line of said Block A to Aransas Bay; Thence [with] the meanders of said Bay to the S. E. corner of said Block A; Thence West with the South boundary line of said Block A to the place of beginning and all rights regarding alley from said land to austin street

and did in said deed retain a Vendor's Lien on the property so Granted, Sold and Conveyed, to secure the payment of a part of the purchase money mentioned in said deed as follows, to-wit: _$5000 00_ _evidenced by two promissory notes of even date with said deed, each in sum of $2500 00, due in 1 & 2 yrs. after date, bearing interest at rate of 8% and payable to order of the_

AND, Whereas, said Vendor's Lien note_s_ given as aforesaid for part purchase money, of said property, ha_ve_ been paid to _the said D. R. Scrivner_ the legal and equitable holder____and owner____of said note_s_;

NOW, THEREFORE, KNOW ALL MEN BY THESE PRESENTS: That _I, D. R. Scrivner_ the present legal and equitable owner____ and holder ___of said Vendor's Lien note _s_ above mentioned, do hereby release, discharge and quitclaim unto the said _Roy Jackson_ heirs and assigns, all the right, title, interest and estate, in and to the property above described which _I have_ to by virtue of being the owner____ of said Vendor's Lien note_s_ and do hereby declare said property released and discharged from any and all liens created by virtue of said Vendor's Lien note _s_ above described.

_2nd_ day of _November_ A.D. 190 _8_

THE STATE OF TEXAS,

COUNTY OF ARANSAS.

This contract, made this 26th day of September, 1942, between Norvell F. Jackson of Aransas County, Texas, who is now in the military service of the United States of America, and who is the owner of the Jackson Sales Company, City of Rockport, Aransas County, Texas, and who is the Consignee of the Texas Company as evidenced by Consignment Agreement, made and entered into by Norvell F. Jackson, Consignee, and the Texas Company, a Delaware Corporation, Consignor, the 1st day of May, 1938, hereinafter referred to as Employer, as one party, and Hugh L. Morrison, of Aransas County, Texas, hereinafter referred to as Manager, as the other party, Witnesseth:

(1) That Employer shall employ Manager for a term beginning on the 1st day of October, 1942, and ending with the discharge of the said Norvell F. Jackson from the Military Service of the United States of America, or as soon thereafter as he can reasonably take over the management of the hereinafter described business, as Manager of the Employer's business as Consignee of the Texas Company and the automobile accessory business known as Jackson Sales Company in the City of Rockport, Aransas County, Texas, subject to determination as hereinafter provided.

(2) The Manager shall well and faithfully serve the Employer in such capacity and shall at all times devote his whole time, attention and energies to the management, superintendence and improvement of the said business, doing and performing all such services and acts connected therewith, and properly belonging to the duties of a manager, which the Employer may from time to time direct. Such services, attentions and acts shall be performed by the Manager to the utmost of his ability.

(3) The Manager shall not divulge any matters relating to the said business or to the Employer or to any customer, which may become

STATE OF TEXAS   ◊

COUNTY OF SAN PATRICIO   ◊   KNOW ALL MEN BY THESE PRESENTS:

That we, S. F. Jackson and wife, Irene Norvell Jackson, herein-

after called Grantor, of Aransas County, Texas, in consideration of

the love and affection which we bear unto our son, Norvell F. Jack-

son of Aransas County, Texas, hereinafter called Grantee, have Grant-

ed, Bargained, Sold and Conveyed and by these presents do Grant,

Bargain, Sell and Convey unto Norvell F. Jackson, said Grantee, as

his sole and separate property, an undivided one-sixth (1/6) interest

in and to all of the oil, gas and other mineral royalties on, in and

under the following described tract of land situated in San Patricio

County, Texas, to-wit:

> Lots One, (1) Two, (2) Three, (3) Four, (4) Seven (7) and
> Eight, (8), and Lots Forty-Three-A (43-A) and Forty-Three-B,
> (43-B) in Section Forty Three (43) of the Fourth (4th) Sub-
> division of the Taft Farm Lands as shown by map of said sub-
> division of record in the office of the County Clerk of San
> Patricio County, Texas, to which reference is here made.

together with the right of ingress and egress at all times for the sole

and only purpose of receiving and removing therefrom the said royalty

oil, gas and other minerals after the same has been produced and saved.

It is distinctly understood and herein stipulated that the above

Sigma Chi

19 ZΠ 73

Texas A&I University

Bill Aldrich

John Alebis

Scott B. Aulds

Conner Bishop

Clifton Brad

Mike Meek
RUSH CHAIRMAN

Bill Barrios
RUSH CHAIRMAN

E. J. Carey
SOCIAL CHAIRMAN

Tommy Power
QUAESTOR

Mike Nemec
CONSUL

Bill Cross

James R. M. Int.
CHAPTER ADVISOR

Mark Ivans

Marly Evans

Bill Kelly

Mike Kriedler

Rick Lisenbe

Scott Lisenbe

Mike McLea

Derryl Phillips

Jim Reed

Bobby Reuther

Bobby Richards

Lynn Sander

Jimmy Campbell

Chuck Carlisle

Craig Carson

Ronnie Corcoran

Mike Benton
PRO-CONSUL

Bobby Jackson
MAGISTER

George Jusica
ANNOTATOR

Allen Jusica
TRIBUNE

Rick Nemec
CHAPTER EDITOR

John Habeeb
KUSTOS

Kenny Brund
SPORTS CHAIRMAN

Jerry DeLay

Alex Harris

Darryl Hazlett

John Hutchinson

Johnny Jackson

Phil Mayeux

David Muir

Tinker Nolan

Mike O'Shea

Larry Slavik

Clark Tatum

Gary Waddell

Gary Wells

George Williams

NOTES AND SOURCES

Since this chronicle has some of the attributes of a memoir, I'm allowed the luxury of recollection, and a personal point of view. Still, I have strived to make the narrative as accurate as possible.

First, I must thank Debbie, for always being there, for sharing her own perspective on our life together, and for helping me unearth the photographs that help bring my narrative to life.

I thank my siblings, Mary Lucille, N.F., and Bobby, who shared memories, documents, and photos; added and corrected information; and sparked my memory.

N.F. provided the photograph of an oil painting of "Riverview," the Norvell family home. The picture was originally published in *William and Mary College Quarterly Historical Magazine*, Vo. 17, page 528.

Bobby supplied the information about Elisha and Irene's employment at the college in Goliad, and about their house on Water Street.

Mary Lucille provided an old newspaper article about the marriage of our grandparents, S.F. Jackson and Irene Norvell.

I give special thanks to my uncle, Bruce Davis, whose prodigious memory and tireless work over many years have provided a rich and detailed history of many branches of the family. His notes supplied a description of S. F. Jackson, and details of his family.

I appreciate Tommy Smith's taking afternoons of his time to talk and remember.

Information on the 1947 fire came from Roy Lassister, David Herring, the *Rockport Pilot*, and the Aransas County centennial booklet. David also confirmed the names of home owners in the early Water Street photo, and figured out that the picture of a group of men must have been taken at Mill's Wharf. (He saw the duck captured by an oyster in the background).

Early parts of our family history were richly described in the chronicles of my great grandmother Irene Barton Norvell, "Nana." I've borrowed heavily from her work.

All photographs and illustrations used are from my collection or the collections of my brothers and sister, unless otherwise noted.

Many of my friends and family contributed their memories to *ARANSAS: The Life of a Texas Coastal County*, by Sue Hastings, with Bill Allen. Their recollections enrich this narrative as well. My thanks go out to them, and to the authors.

I have reproduced portions of two maps that originally appeared in *ARANSAS: The Life of a Texas Coastal County*. Both were drawn by Chris Blum, an artist who lived in Rockport in 1997, when that book was published.

Perry Richardson Bass, a supporter of that book, and an important figure in my life story, died on June 1, 2006, at the age of 91. He was widely known as oil man, financier, philanthropist and environmentalist.

Information on the early fish houses came from a 1939 newspaper interview with D. R. Scrivner, an interview with Marion Johnson, my uncle Bruce Davis' family history, and the Aransas County Centennial booklet.

Some information on shrimp and early shrimping came from a pamphlet produced by the Texas Parks and Wildlife Department and from an article in *Aransas Pass, Texas*.

Some information regarding fisheries and the EEZ came from "Economic Impact of Mexico's 200-mile Offshore Fishing Zone on the United States Gulf of Mexico Shrimp Fishery, by Wade L. Griffin and Bruce R. Beattie. http://www.jstor.org/pss/3146200

Today, 90% of shrimp caught are brown shrimp, from the Gulf. But in the early days, according to my father, Norvell Jackson, there was no market for them. People believed that a brown shrimp was a spoiled shrimp. They weren't familiar with brown shrimp, which came into the bays only for May and June. The rest of the time, brown shrimp were in Gulf waters too deep for bay shrimpers to go after them. Because of the myth, and the inaccessibility, there was no viable Gulf shrimp fishery for many years.

Female blue crabs molt 18-20 times in a lifetime; males 20-23 times. Information from: www.bluecrab.info

Information on the School Land Board came from "The Handbook of Texas Online." http://www.tshaonline.org/handbook/online/articles/PP/khp1.html

On January 28, 1942, *The Rockport Pilot* wrote that Floyd Huffman and Norvell Jackson had been named air raid observers atop the courthouse.

The Rockport Pilot, June 27, 1963, provided details of Irene Norvell Jackson's community activities.

In the *Corpus Christi Caller-Times*, July 14, 1963, Sue Smith's interview with Irene Norvell Jackson has provided helpful information on her activities, and also on "Old Rockport" as she remembered it.

The Handbook of Texas Online provided information on Vietnam refugees in the area.

My thanks to Lewis Robinson for allowing me to reproduce his vision of development for Rockport Harborfront.